When God Sent Grace
to the
Soviet Gulag

One Man's Incredible Journey to Freedom

Andrew Mytych

When God Sent Grace to the Soviet Gulag
© 2013, Andrzej (Andrew) Mytych

www.andrzejmytych.pl

Originally Published in Polish 2011
By Andrzej Mytych

English Translation
by Jerry Dean

Edited by
Eileen Daigle

Cover Design
Jeff Daigle

Contact for Distribution
World Missions Advance
PO Box 764408
Dallas, TX 75376
Tel. 972-709-9900
info@worldmissionsadvance.org
www.worldmissionsadvance.org

ISBN: 978-1493550678

ISBN: 1493550675

What we have heard and known,
What our fathers have told us.
We will not hide them from their children;
We will tell the next generation.

Psalm 78:3-4 (NIV)

Table of Contents

FORWARD

The powerful testimonies of the Kiewra family and the roads that were taken and ordained by God will touch the hearts of all who read their story. This book documents the events of one man's journey of obedience in the midst of the harshest realities. This testimony does not stop with him. His personal impact on one young man, in particular, is documented and reveals his ongoing influence to generations. The story details the provision of God in circumstances that would make the strongest of us question God's purposes in such suffering.

I can enthusiastically recommend this book as a source of encouragement and faith strengthening for the personal journey anyone may be walking.

Susan Bozarth

President, World Missions Advance

Dallas, Texas

The Story Behind the Book

The idea of writing the book

The idea of writing the book, *When God Sent Grace to the Soviet Gulag*, was born in my heart during a trip to Belarus in September of 2008. One day during the trip, I was listening to my pastor Marek (Mark) Kiewra telling the story of the political imprisonment and then the labor-camp conversion of his father, Cezary Kiewra. I previously had talked to Cezary about the concentration camps of the Soviet Gulag and Christianity during this difficult period in Polish/Eastern European history. But when I heard the story from his son, I decided that it needed to be written down to prevent its being lost in oblivion.

As we flew back to Poland, I told Marek that we should write a book about his father. Cezary's life was passing, and it would be a shame if the story passed away with him. Marek initially agreed, but said that he had to think about it some more.

Conversations with Kiewra family

Sometime later, I was invited to the Kiewra home to further discuss with family members the writing of the book about Cezary. In general, they liked the idea—only Cezary and his wife, Łucja, told me that, in their view, it made no sense to write such a book because they are simple people and their life story is not material for a book. Łucja doubted that anyone would be interested. It was difficult to agree with her point of view. After a long conversation, we agreed that I should start the work but that the account should be written in a concise manner, meaning that it could be read in three hours.

Writing the book

Over the next few years, I found more people who knew the story. The hardest part was to find the relatives of Aurel Serafinczan, the Gulag-imprisoned pastor who became the mentor and lifelong friend of Cezary. We found them "by accident." One time Marek Kiewra was in a Russian-speaking church in Atlanta, Georgia (USA). It turned out that some of the people in the Atlanta church came from Chernivtsi, Ukraine, from the church where Aurel had been one of the leaders. They gave Marek a phone number for the grandson of Vasyl Serafinczan, Aurel's brother. I called him on the phone and a few weeks later, in May 2010, I went to Ukraine to interview Aurel's relatives and friends. It was a very interesting trip, and Vasyl turned out to be a fascinating man. I spent a few days at his house and also visited the gravesite of Aurel who died in 1997.

Vasyl said that many people had requested interviews with him, but he never agreed. However, he said because he knew Cezary, he would make an exception and talk to me. He requested, however, that I would not change anything in what he said. He insisted that I should write the story exactly as he told it.

I ended up with over 60 audio files from Ukraine as well as old photographs taken in Siberia. Then came the laborious part of listening to the audio files, writing down what was said in the interviews, and putting the story together.

Fictionalize or not?

I began writing the book in 2011. For some time, Marek Kiewra, his wife Wanda, and I wondered if the book should be fictionalized. But, in the end, we gave up on this idea. We decided to leave the material as it was described by witnesses of the story. The actual account would prove to be "stranger than fiction"!

So, we left a "raw" text which is a record of interviews with witnesses of the events. Even the dialogues presented in the book were not invented by me but came from interviews.

Why I wrote the book

I wrote it for several reasons:

First of all, I was asked many times by my friends to write this story.

Secondly, as previously mentioned, I believe that this story deserves to be protected from passing into oblivion. Too many stories of this kind have died with the death of the main characters.

Thirdly, this book fills a gap in our literature about the Evangelicals in post-war communist Poland. I hope that others will follow in my footsteps and begin to create this type of literature. Otherwise, our knowledge and experience will die with us though it is our common heritage which should be preserved and passed on to future generations.

Finally, although the book describes the events of several decades which occurred in a different period and culture, they show universal truth about God who finds a faithful man and about another man who experiences a transforming encounter with God. It teaches us a lot about the grace of our Lord.

Some personal notes....

I am glad that this book has been written and published. While working on the biography of Cezary Kiewra, I had the privilege to get to know him personally while spending a few months with him and his wife talking about their lives. I must admit that I was fascinated by the simplicity yet depth of their history. They took me on a journey to a time and a world that no longer exist but, by all means, deserved to be described and preserved.

1

A Difficult Childhood

The turmoil of war

The dramatic separation from his father

There was a time when the insane vision of conquering the whole world was born in the heart of Adolf Hitler, the leader of the Third Reich. The attempted realization of that goal caused great tragedy in the lives of those completely ill-prepared for what awaited them. It began on the morning of September 1, 1939, when the German army attacked the Republic of Poland. That attack was only the beginning of the largest conflict in the history of mankind–the Second World War–and thus began the unspeakable suffering of millions.

The turmoil of war touched everyone, reaching also a small, sleepy village called Wikszniany ("Veeksh-NYAH-nih") in what were called the Eastern Borderlands of Poland at that time. Thirty-five-year-old Nikodem Kiewra ("Nee-KO-dem KYEV-rah") gathered his whole family into his home in order to say goodbye. It was an especially moving moment, even though the children had no idea what was happening, for they could not understand the seriousness of the situation.

Pain tore at Nikodem's heart. He cried intensely because he knew that his family had to cope with the unforeseen situation in which they found themselves. He picked up his eldest son Cezary ("seh-ZAH-rih"), only 9 years old at the time, and placed him on a stool. Through his tears, he looked straight into his child's eyes and said, "Son, you're the oldest here. I am leaving...." He paused for a moment, and then asked, "Son, when will we meet again?"

The moment of bidding farewell to his family was full of emotion and tenderness. Because of his conscription into military service as an army reservist, Nikodem had to leave those closest to him in the graces of the ever-nearing turmoil of war. Brokenhearted, he did not know what fate would bring him, his wife, or their four small sons.

Cezary, looking at his loving dad who was a great authority in his life, had no idea that they would be reunited only after 26 long years, in faraway England! But such was the downturn of the summer of 1939. That tumultuous time brought fear, anxiety, and the pain of parting into Polish homes. No one knew what was coming. Additionally, no one expected that history would move in such an evil direction, carrying along with it thousands of Polish families, among them the Kiewra family–simple, but wise peasants from a sleepy little village in Eastern Poland.

Cezary's Parents

Nikodem was born in 1904 in the village of Wikszniany. It was here he spent his childhood and youth. His parents were peasants.

In 1927, he married Wiktoria Dubicka ("Veek-TOH-ria Doo-BEETS-ka") who was three years younger than he and who came from a better-situated family from Potasznia ("Poh-TASH-nya"), about 12½ miles from Wikszniany. Their wedding was held in the neighboring town of Iwje ("EEV-yeh") because the village of Wikszniany was so small that it didn't even have its own church.

When Wiktoria arrived in Wikszniany after her wedding and saw where she would be living, she all but fainted from the impression it made. For several days she was depressed because Nikodem lived in a wood cottage that was falling apart. And instead of a wooden floor, it had a clay, earthen floor. The site of her beloved, who daily walked about in long shirts tied off with cord, also did not suit the tastes of the young wife.

Thankfully, Nikodem was an intelligent, good, and hard-working man. He had learned blacksmithing and, in his simplicity and dedication, he desired to give his wife the best standard of living possible. After their wedding, he built their own small forge, pigpen, and barn as well as a new wooden home on cement foundations. It was the only one of its type in the whole village! In the house, they had a spacious kitchen and one room which fulfilled the functions of both a living room and bedroom. Close to their home, they had a little over six acres of beautiful land near a forest, with picturesque apple orchards and a well.

Wiktoria was now a normal, simple, village woman who worked on a farm. In time, she gave birth to four sons–the oldest was Cezary, born on March 1, 1931. After him, Janek ("YAH-nek"), May 7, 1933; Wiktor ("VEEK-tor"), June 11, 1935; and Adam, March 15, 1938.

Nikodem provided the discipline in the home and Wiktoria, in her humility of heart and out of her sincere love for her children, gave herself to taking care of their sons. Nikodem instilled a sense of responsibility for their home into all of the family members. A "whip," consisting of a wooden handle with thongs attached to the end, helped to keep discipline among the boys. If they misbehaved, the "whip" went into action.

Wartime childhood

When Nikodem left for war, Cezary was only 9 years old. A year earlier, Cezary had begun Polish school and finished first grade. However, in the fall of 1939, he could not continue learning Polish because on September 17th (2 weeks after the German invasion), the Soviet army unexpectedly attacked Poland. The Soviet army crossed the eastern borders of the country, declaring that they were coming as friends. The Polish people had no knowledge of the secret pact between Stalin and Hitler which guaranteed non-aggression between those two countries. The secret agreement was signed on August 23, 1939, and is called the Ribbentrop-Molotov pact, derived from the last names of the respective ministers of foreign affairs. No one then, and not even many years later, had any knowledge about the secret protocols in which Poland was partitioned and its territories divided.

And so, in September of 1939, Poland was attacked from two sides. First, the Fascists attacked from the West and the North and, 17 days later, the Soviets attacked from the East. The first military actions of the war by Poland were short-lived and ended in catastrophe for the Poles. As a result of those losses, part of the country found itself under German control and occupation while the other came under Soviet control. In reality, this meant that the western part of the country experienced the cruelty of Nazi totalitarianism while the eastern part suffered under Soviet totalitarianism.

After September 17th, the village of Wikszniany came under Soviet occupation. Cezary had to continue his education in a Soviet school. Byelorussian was spoken on a daily basis in the village, while Russian was spoken in school. He would finish just four classes of elementary school, three of which were completely held in Russian.

When Nikodem Kiewra went to war, Cezary, as the eldest son in the family, had to take on part of the responsibilities around the house. He remembered the chaos of war, as did thousands of other children, as a time of hunger and cold. In their home, they had a single pair of shoes which the four boys had to take turns wearing. Regardless of the season, the boys walked barefoot. Especially in the winter months, frozen feet caused intense pain. In order to warm their frozen feet, the brothers would often insert them into cow dung. Even in the summer, when Cezary would lead the cows to pasture early in the morning, treading on grass infused with the morning dew caused him great pain.

To insure her family's well-being, Wiktoria took care of two cows and worked hard in the fields, often taking her children with her. In order to keep them busy, she gave them a "sugar tit," a mixture of bread and sugar wrapped in a rag, to suck on.

Cezary was a capable and resourceful child. In order to help his mother, he worked in the forge braiding baskets. He made graters and other items that were helpful, not only in the kitchen but elsewhere. Later, he traded out his handiwork for flour, bread, groats (whole-grains of wheat, oats, or barley), and eggs. People living in the village treated Cezary with great respect, calling him a "Wise Solomon," because he was a talented and resourceful little "craftsman." Cezary did not know who Solomon was, but he assumed that by calling him that, the villagers were paying him a compliment.

Wiktoria's parents, Michał ("MEEK-how") and Aniela ("Ah-NYEH-lah"), moved into the house built by Nikodem in order to help their daughter and grandchildren survive the years of war.

On June 22, 1941, the Third Reich attacked the Soviet Union, executing the so-called "Operation Barbarossa." The war front moved toward the East. So, in a short amount of time, the Third Reich consumed the peaceful village of Wikszniany. The reality of living in a war zone and the approach of fascism wrapped Cezary in fear. In order to survive, the Kiewra family hid. But it was impossible to find a peaceful place at that time. The surrounding towns were bombed, houses burned, and people filled with fear simply tried to survive without getting killed.

During the German occupation, Cezary's family had the two cows. German soldiers regularly took all "surplus" food from the peasants. A few of them were shot when they refused to hand over their food because they were trying to keep it for their loved ones. Cezary remembered the shooting of his neighbors, the extermination of the Jews in nearby cities and forests, as well as the nameless, unmarked mass graves called "brotherhood graves."

One day, German soldiers on one of the roads came under attack by Soviet partisans. As an act of revenge, the soldiers decided to take out their frustration on the inhabitants of a nearby village which lay about 2 miles from Wikszniany. They proclaimed that its villagers helped the partisans. Some of the village inhabitants were shot immediately while the fascists forced others into a barn where they were then burned alive. The German soldiers did not show mercy to anyone. They murdered small children, teenagers, women, and the elderly–everyone who fell into their hands.

The most horrible of memories

Especially close to Cezary's heart was the family of an elderly Jewish shoe maker who was well respected in Wikszniany. He sewed and repaired the shoes of several generations of village residents. He had two beautiful daughters whose hands had not yet been given in marriage. Cezary was especially close to Raisa, his school teacher. He loved to paint horses and other animals, which were part of his daily surroundings. And, because he drew so well, she often encouraged him to dedicate one of his many pictures to her.

Unfortunately, the war with its barbarity was thrust onto the lives of an ever-growing number of people and reaped a massive harvest of death. The leaders of the Third Reich had decided to limit unwanted populations and transform them into a slave force, so they singled out certain ethnic groups. The Jews awaited *complete extermination*. The Germans went about realizing their plans with deadly precision. The Jews were hunted, robbed, placed in ghettos, and systematically exterminated.

One ghetto of this type was created in the town of Iwje ("EEV-yeh"), located nearby Wikszniany (and the town in which Nikodem and Wiktoria had been married).The German army entered that town on July 1, 1941, and immediately ordered all of its citizens to return to their homes and not leave. The Germans allowed the town's inhabitants to plunder their Jewish neighbors for four days. Some neighbors who, up until this point, had lived together with Jews in peace and harmony plundered the Jewish homes in broad daylight. In one of the homes, even a small baby was robbed of its blanket. Ironically, a German commander and his officers stopped these four days of violence and lawlessness when they arrived.

Jewish men were beaten by the Germans and forced to work. As the war progressed, the Gestapo began the progressive liquidation of the Jewish people, starting with the intellectuals, Communists, and youth.

Shortly, all the Jews of Iwje and the surrounding towns were gathered into one place. The Germans robbed them of what was left, and then the real carnage began. Thousands of Jews were murdered in cold blood in Stoniewicze ("Stoh-nyeh-VEE-cheh"). Dug-out ditches were filled with the bodies of 4,000 people. Their clothes were then sold for half price in the local stores.

People would tell of strange and horrible things that happened during these mass murders. One story is told of two Jews who lost their minds. For whatever reason, the German soldiers allowed them to leave the mass grave site. In bewilderment and completely out of touch with reality, they walked arm-in-arm back to their village which was 2 miles from the site, singing Jewish songs all the way.

Some of the wounded were buried alive because the Germans did not *kill* the wounded who were shot before filling in the grave. The ground moved for three more days and three nights after the massacre. And from beneath the ground, the ghostlike cries of the dying could be heard. It is said that the hair on the heads of the locals stood on end because of the horrible sounds coming out of the earth. Witnesses stated that blood flowed to the surface and coagulated between the furrows. The remaining Jews, between 1,200 and 1,300 people, were sent to a ghetto and, after two months, the killings started again.

Altogether, 5,000 Jews died. For Cezary, that was the most horrible story that took place at the time. The Kiewra family was deeply hurt by the fact that Poles also caused those people to suffer. Raisa, Cezary's favorite teacher, her sister, and her father also died together with those whose lives were ended in such a brutal way. Cezary was never able to make sense of, or come to terms with, those losses.

The wartime fate of Nikodem

After mobilization in the summer of 1939, Nikodem Kiewra, Cezary's father, was sent to defend the city of Lviv ("Luh-VEEF"), which was an important city and part of eastern Poland at that time. However, despite many days of regular fighting, the city fell. The soldiers of the Polish Army, fighting against the Germans, were forced by the Bolsheviks (Russian Communists) to lay down their arms and were taken as prisoners of war.

When the Third Reich later broke its pact with Russia and attacked the U.S.S.R., Polish-Soviet relations reversed. Under a decree of amnesty for Polish citizens, Nikodem was released. At this time, the Soviet army was experiencing heavy losses, so they needed new soldiers to fill its ranks. Joseph Stalin then declared the Great Patriotic War in order to encourage as many people to fight against the Germans as possible. As it turned out, he would need the Poles, as well.

Together with thousands of other men, Nikodem joined the Polish divisions under the command of General Władysław ("vwah-DIH-swaf") Anders. They quickly realized that they were seriously lacking officers. A harsh reality came to light—most of the officers had been murdered by the Soviets in the forest around Katyn, in Kharkiv, and Mednoye (cities in the USSR at that time). The fact of the murder of Polish officers, in conjunction with the difficulty related to equipping the Polish armed forces, led to a serious crisis in Polish-Soviet relations and caused General Anders to lead his Polish divisions, formed in the USSR, to the Middle East in 1942.

For several years, Nikodem's fate was tied to the Anders' 2nd Corps, also called "Anders' Army." As a corporal, he served as a supply clerk. Together with that corps, he followed an amazing road from the Middle East, through Africa, in order to end up finally fighting on the Italian front.

Nikodem doesn't return home

Cezary loved his father very much and missed him dearly. He was emotionally connected to his dad and, throughout his childhood, was hurt by his lack of a father. With the passing of the years, that pain intensified. However, for political reasons, Nikodem would not return home.

Cezary wrote his father a letter in which he inserted a black and white photograph of himself. On the back of the picture he wrote, "Don't forget me, Dad!"

During the defense over the Sangro River in Italy, the battle for Monte Cassino, as well as other battles, the soldiers of the 2nd Corps stood out for their extraordinary bravery. However, their successes were bought at a great loss of life. Many soldiers close to Nikodem died in various battles and confrontations. These painful experiences remained forever in his memory, but he knew he had to learn to live in those kinds of circumstances and somehow look to the future with hope.

Nikodem showed himself to be a great patriot and a man of principles. Just as did many of his brothers-in-arms, he held to four pre-war Polish values which he would recite in the following order: God, Honor, Fatherland, and Family.

The soldiers of the 2nd Corps went with Anders and fought with dedication because they trusted him and believed that they would see a free Poland. With time, however, it became apparent that fate cruelly mocked them. At the end of the war, the leaders of the United States, Great Britain, and the Soviet Union met a few times. Winston Churchill, Franklin Roosevelt, and Joseph Stalin decided in Yalta that Poland would lose its Eastern border lands to the Soviet Union. The USSR, or "the Union of Soviet Socialist Republics," received "authority" over Poland and one-third of Germany, whereas Poland, as compensation for its losses, was given land that, up to that time, had belonged to Germany: Western Pomerania, East Prussia, and the Silesia region, along with its complicated history.

Moscow imposed its regime on Poland, appointing it a puppet government. As a result of such a decision, General Anders urged his soldiers not to return to their country since Communists were ruling it. *"Poland has become a Communist country. Therefore, choose whatever country you want. Please, just don't return to Communist Poland."*

The soldiers of Anders' army did not need further explanation because many of them had experienced first-hand the "Gehenna" of the Soviet regime. Many of those gathered had been serving sentences in the Gulag's camps or had been in exile before joining the 2nd Corps. They did not, therefore, have any illusions as to the real nature of communism.

For that reason, many of Anders' soldiers decided not to return to their homes. Some of them immigrated to various countries. Nikodem also decided not to return to his family village. He figured that returning to a Soviet Wikszniany would be unwise because Communists are unpredictable. He desired to be close to his family, but he also wanted to be far enough away from the totalitarian Soviet Union. For that reason, he decided to immigrate to Great Britain. Later, his fears turned out to be justified completely. In 1951, close to 4,500 of Anders' soldiers, called "Andersons," who returned to their family homes in Belarus, Lithuania, and Ukraine were arrested (together with their families) and deported to Siberia.

In Great Britain, Nikodem settled in Bradford where there was a large concentration of Poles. Because he was a good builder, specializing in remodeling, he began that kind of business upon arrival. He especially enjoyed repairing chimneys, roofs, and gutters. Part of the *Andersons*, who stayed on "the Island" as immigrants, decided to start life again and form new families. For Nikodem, this was unthinkable! He was faithful to his wife and believed unwaveringly that, one day, he would manage to bring his whole family to Great Britain to live with him. He kept contact with them through correspondence and sent part of the money he made for their living expenses back home.

Cezary chooses a tailor's trade

Cezary was a capable and intelligent boy. When he turned 15, his mother sent him to work as a tailor's apprentice so that he could learn the trade. For two years, until December of 1947, he worked as an assistant to an experienced village tailor. (Cezary had begun sewing much earlier and, looking at his handiwork, one would realize that he had a natural talent for the trade.) He added pockets to pants and sewed hats, which he later sold, using the money to support his family.

Together with his teacher, he traveled from house to house. They put the sewing machine on their backs and walked to whatever village the client lived in. Whenever people needed a tailor's services, they would invite the tailor and assistant (if there was one) into their home. During that time, they would be guaranteed food and a roof over their heads. They sewed with a machine as well as manually made clothing repairs. They also created a myriad of items, including coats and furs. It was tedious and difficult work, and their fingers would swell from the pressure of the needles after sewing by hand, especially furs.

At 17 years of age, Cezary had his *own* student named Wiktor ("VEEK-tor"), and he could become independent from his "master." He stopped working from house to house and began sewing in one place in Wikszniany, where his clients began to come to him.

Cezary was well liked in his village for several different reasons. He skillfully used his abilities to repair or create many items needed on a daily basis. As a sought-after tailor, he also had money. And beyond that, he was sociable and the master of ceremonies at village dances that he organized in various homes in his village.

He worked as a tailor, as well as helping his family on the family farm, until the age of 19. He remembered his youth as a happy one. Unfortunately, the carefree life did not last very long because in September of 1950, he was arrested and, six months later, sent to a labor camp.

Poland on the world map. August 31, 1939

Polish territory absorbed by the Third Reich and the Soviet Union

Nikodem and Wiktoria on their wedding day

Nikodem Kiewra (first from the left) in Anders' 2nd Corp, Palestine

Nikodem Kiewra in Bradford, October 1, 1950

Cezary (on the right) with his apprentice

On the back of the photo is written:

"Don't forget about me, Dad!"

Andrew Mytych

2

Exile to the North

When Stalin's labor camp becomes a paradise

The arrest and sentence

At the end of World War II, when the front moved toward Berlin, some residents gathered weapons and ammunition left behind after the war. The Germans left some of these things near Juraciszki ("Yoo-ra-CHEESH-kee") after withdrawing in a hurry in 1944 before the Soviet Army reached them. The weapons were seized and hid by local peasants. In the woods opposite his house, Cezary found a German machine gun with a damaged magazine. He also managed to gather some hand grenades and bullets. He carefully wrapped the machine gun and bullets and buried them in the nearby woods under the cover of night.

In order to protect themselves, some people acted this way because the times were uncertain and troubled. The borders of the nation shifted, and the war front moved back and forth in each direction. In those unsettled areas, different formations of partisans operated, and ethnic cleansing took place. Bands of common criminals also moved about. Because of these things, people tried to ensure a little bit of safety. They thought that maybe they would need to defend themselves, fight, or even "settle the score" with someone.

(As an aside, Cezary discovered another interesting use for hand grenades. Every now and then he traveled to the village where his uncle and grandfather lived. Through this small, charming village flowed the Brzoza River. Cezary got a rather shocking idea to throw hand grenades into the water and stun the fish which he then could easily scoop out with a net.)

Five years later, in 1950, some of the Polish partisans who had been a part of the Home Army arrived in Cezary's village. They were now fighting against the Soviet authorities in the underground structure of the former Home Army. Quietly, they asked peasants about hidden weapons and ammunition. Under their insistence, Cezary betrayed the place where a few years before he had hidden the machine gun and ammunition. Although the machine gun was defective, they took everything they could get their hands on. "Who knows," they said, "anything can come in handy!"

Former Home Army partisans operating in the area were engaged in propaganda and believed that they were fighting for the restoration of the land for the Poles. In addition, they defended the people residing there from bandits. The Soviet authorities had a completely different opinion about them. They took the underground army to be criminals who should be eliminated. Of course, from their point of view, these allegations were justified because the partisans killed Soviet officers and officials.

The job of eliminating the underground partisans on the western terrain of the Soviet Union was given to the MGB, the Soviet's Ministry for State Security, which dealt with counter-intelligence and fighting against the internal enemies of the Soviet regime. Until 1953, the MGB effectively destroyed divisions of Polish partisans derived from Home Army structures. The fight against them contributed to the increase of Soviet terror against the Polish population living in these areas.

It was during this critical period that Cezary supplied Polish partisans with the machine gun and ammunition. It just so happened that Soviet counterintelligence arrested a group of these partisans. During interrogation, they betrayed everyone they knew, including 19-year-old Cezary, which resulted in his immediate arrest. First, the officials took him to the prison in a city near Minsk, the capital of Belarus, where an investigation was conducted against him for several months. A constant element of the investigation was interrogation, during which Cezary stubbornly refused to admit guilt. He was in a cell with a man who, sometime later, said to Cezary after he was dragged back unconscious from the interrogation:

"Listen, just because you're stubborn and you don't admit to guilt, it doesn't help you. After all, they have already collected accusing testimony about you. Don't be stupid. They won't let you sleep. They'll torture you until you confess. After all, your situation is hopeless. Boy, you already have one foot in the labor camps, even if you do not realize it yet. You are going to confess anyway, and they will give you 25 years in the camps. That's for sure. Is there any sense in going through unnecessary torture?"

Cezary, in order to prevent torture, eventually admitted that he delivered weapons hidden during World War II to the Polish underground.

On December 8, 1950, a trial was held. Together with three other Poles, Cezary was tried for *providing food, alcohol, as well as weapons and ammunition* to Polish partisans. Cezary's "criminal" activity—providing the partially-damaged machine gun and ammunition in April 1950.... All four pleaded guilty, and the military tribunal convicted them. Cezary was sentenced to 25 years in labor camps and the confiscation of all of his property. This was the punishment for helping *Polish bandits and conducting subversive activities against the government and the Soviet regime.* The decision was handed down on December 22, 1950, and the judgment was considered final.

After the verdict, Cezary was transferred to the transitional prison in Orsha. From there, convicts were sent to labor camps deep inside the Soviet Union, according to the demand for labor. In March 1951 (almost one year after being taken prisoner), Cezary and other prisoners were loaded into a freight car, not having any idea where they were going. Immediately, the entire Kiewra farm was valued by Soviet officials, and Cezary's mother had to pay the government her son's part of it.

The journey to Siberia

There was nothing in the freight car except a hole chopped out by an ax that served as a primitive toilet. The car was not heated, in spite of the fact that the temperature was still very cold. So, packed like sardines, people slept on the floor of the train car, side by side, warming each other with their bodies. They received meager food rations—water and dry bread. This inhumane journey lasted two weeks.

During one of the stops, someone brought their daily portion and mockingly said, "Drink water and get fat."

The longer they traveled, the colder it got. There is no way to imagine how penetrating and unbearable the cold was! Wagons without any heat, with ice on the outside and inside, carried many people to certain death. One day Cezary asked, "Why is it so terribly cold? After all, it's March. It should be much warmer." A Russian prisoner replied, "We are going far north. That's why it has become so cold."

Some deportees died on the journey during the days and others, at night. The surviving prisoners would realize in the mornings that the bodies of their companions were frozen. The dead were thrown into the surrounding wilderness by the convicts and soldiers on the train. The deceased, without any type of funeral, were absorbed by the snowy vastness. Only the silence of the surviving, frozen prisoners bid them farewell.

Cezary survived this terrible trip only because he had a young and strong body. Finally, after 14 days that stretched into what seemed like an eternity, they reached their destination. When the prisoners came out of the freight car, they wanted to know where they were. They heard, "Komi ASSR." They lost all hope. It was the end of the world.

Komi ASSR and the Gulag

Komi Autonomous Soviet Socialist Republic, known as "Komi ASSR," lay on the western side of the Ural Mountains in the northeastern part of Russia. The Republic was, and still is, sparsely populated. More than half of this area, part of the Siberian *taiga* (vast forest lands), is untouched by human hands. In addition, a relatively large area of the republic is mud.

Before the war, rich deposits of coal, oil, natural gas, gold, and diamonds were discovered in Komi. This region became an important point on the industrial map of the Soviet Union as well as an important part of the Soviet economy. In the 1930s, industry was created on this virgin land. The construction of railways and roads began, and the development of industrial projects required hundreds of thousands of workers who would work in inhumane conditions. Few wanted to voluntarily work there, so labor camps were organized in that Republic to ensure the needed infrastructure.

The *Gulag* (*GULag,* acronym for *Chief Administration of Corrective Labor Camps and Colonies*) was nothing more than a penal system of forced labor camps in the USSR. They were the Soviet version of concentration camps. In the camps, tens of millions of people performed slave labor for the Soviet economy. A large part of them were Poles, sent deep into Russia from Polish lands that were seized by the Soviet Union starting in the autumn of 1939.

The labor camps became the symbol of Stalinist terror and totalitarianism, as well as an image of innocent suffering and human cruelty. Criminal offenders and "socially-undesirable persons" (those publicly suspected in the light of Soviet legislation) were sent to them.

The network of labor camps was huge. It consisted of several thousand camps spread throughout the Soviet Union. The living conditions were similar to German concentration camps. The primary objective of the camps was "re-education through labor," but many of them were nothing more than a place of extermination through slave labor. It is estimated that by 1956, about 50 million people might have been killed in such conditions.

In 1951, at the age of 20, Cezary Kiewra, a tailor from a tiny village of Wikszniany, arrived at Komi ASSR. This Polish boy was brought to this far north land to be "re-educated" into a "decent Soviet citizen." He came with a sentence of 25 years which, in the case of many convicts, meant death. As a "welcome" to the labor camp, he heard a word from one of the prisoners which indicated a terrifying future: "Cezary, here you only leave carried out feet first!" First, he was sent to a camp where prisoners worked clearing the *taiga* and building roads leading to drilling towers. In Komi ASSR were very rich deposits of crude oil, but significant problems stemmed from the lack of a transportation infrastructure. It prohibited the full extraction of this wealth that was very much needed for the rapidly-developing industry of the Soviet Union back then. Labor camps were created strategically which allowed trees (cut down by the prisoners) and sand to be used to build roads. In this labor camp, Cezary spent one and a half years working on roads. At the place of work, food rations were brought which consisted of water and square pieces of hardened porridge. In the mornings before work and in the evenings after returning, he received soup and a piece of bread.

Sometimes packages with dry provisions came to the labor camp. When such a package came to a prisoner, he needed to share. Otherwise, he was immediately robbed. If someone went to complain to the camp authorities, he heard this response: "So, what? If you did not eat it, someone else did. This is the Soviet Union. Here we have everything in common. You need to share."

The camp was composed of many barracks, and a thick pipe (welded on one side) led to each one which provided heat to these makeshift buildings. The camp was built on huge deposits of natural gas which was the way the convicts' barracks were heated. On this pipe prisoners dried their belongings that got wet during work. The stench was unbelievable and permeated everything. In each barrack, 25 to 30 people slept on bunk beds.

Some prisoners made a desperate attempt to escape. (During Cezary's stay in the Gulag system, no one got away.) If someone managed to escape, it was difficult to survive alone on this inhumane, vast, and sparsely-populated land without anyone's help. Sooner or later, fugitives were caught and placed in solitary confinement. Some of them were shot immediately, and those wounded by bullets in the chase or bitten by dogs were thrown into the penalty cell.

In this camp, no one cared for the convicts. There were no doctors or medicines. Those weak and sick simply died.

Prisoners, seeking to survive in these punitive conditions, were overcome with powerlessness and helplessness. There was a boy who was very well liked by all. He was arrested as a teenager and worked for several years in various labor camps. At one point, after losing all hope of returning to a normal life, he decided to put an end to his fate. He had access to explosives used in construction. One day, when filled with so much hopelessness and despair, he gathered some small explosives, wrapped them around his head, and detonated them. His companions were shocked and deeply saddened.

Cezary, young and strong and determined, survived. After 18 months of clearing the *taiga*, he was transferred to mining oil.

Strange prisoner

In August 1952, Cezary and a group of prisoners were sent to a labor camp known as *Camp AA-2*, located by an oil mine. Every day he worked at a depth of 790 feet under the ground, drilling horizontal boreholes. Through these openings, transparent oil was mined, which the convicts called *white oil*. The prisoners worked in difficult and dangerous conditions as large deposits of methane accompanied the oil deposits. At any moment, the deportees could lose their lives due to an explosion of gas.

The working conditions in the mine were so difficult that if a prisoner fulfilled his duties well, two or three days were taken off from his sentence for every one-day's work.

Cezary was pleased that he was moved from the *taiga* to this labor camp because here, the prisoners were better fed. Better food meant that there was more dry bread, and each morning and evening they had soup.

❧ ❧ ❧ ❧ ❧

One day, a transport with prisoners from the labor camp in Ukhta arrived at the camp. One prisoner really stood out because of his quite unusual behavior. He was a tall, handsome, and well-built Romanian, approximately 30 years old. His name was Aurel Serafinczan ("seh-ra-FEEN-chan").

His attitude was incomprehensible because, in spite of the circumstances that they were in, at all times he was happy and thanked God for everything. He quickly became known among the prisoners because he did something that no one else ever did: When he received his bread portion, he prayed over it and divided it into several portions. One portion he ate, and the rest he gave away. His attitude to life in the camp and his approach to people provoked astonishment among the convicts.

It was something unthinkable! One of the worst things that prisoners experienced doing hard labor was chronic hunger. They worked very hard in difficult conditions and received very little food. Cezary felt hungry all the time. Hunger! Hunger! Hunger! At night, hunger! During the day, hunger! There were nights that he dreamed of bread. He saw how the bread was being baked. He smelled the wonderful aroma that spread throughout the room of freshly-baked, crunchy bread. He dreamed of holding a hot loaf in his hands. How the pleasant aroma stimulated the sense of smell when he broke it! How the warm bread melted in his mouth when he took a bite of it! But when he awoke, he only had rumblings in his stomach. Again, hunger! And the Romanian? What was *he* doing? He gave away his own bread!

Furthermore, he smiled all the time and often pulled out some small pieces of paper from his pockets, paper somewhat resembling that used for rolling cigarettes. He read them. Reading them apparently caused him great pleasure because the whole time, he smiled to himself.

In the mine, no one was happy. People rarely smiled. What can you be happy about in a Siberian labor camp?

Cezary became more intrigued by this strange Romanian. So, one day he overcame his curiosity and went to him. "My name is Cezary," introducing himself with a certain confident tone. "I am a Pole. And who you are?"

"My name is Aurel. I am a Romanian from Bucovina," he responded, looking curiously at Cezary. Cezary cast his eyes on the small papers that Aurel had in his hand.

"What's that? What are you reading all the time?"

"This is a fragment from the Holy Bible. As you read it, your life begins to change," he replied.

"I am Catholic," declared Cezary, and he took the rosary out of his pocket. "I say the rosary to the Mother of God so that she will take care of me. Besides that, I always carry with me a sacred image." At that point, he took from his pocket a picture of a saint.

"So, I meet a kindred spirit!" Aurel smiled from ear to ear. "I see that you are a godly man. Maybe this is a good time to deepen your faith by reading the Holy Bible."

"Ah, yeah, but why?" Cezary made a puzzled face. "After all, I already have my rosary."

"You have the rosary, but do you understand your faith?" asked Aurel. "Start to read the Holy Bible. God Himself speaks through this book and teaches us how to direct our lives and live according to it."

"Maybe some other time," answered Cezary. He lit a cigarette and left.

In the camps, those in charge looked for wise and capable prisoners in order to give them various duties. When Cezary had worked in the mine for about a year, he became a foreman, and Aurel was designated as his assistant. At that time, the 20-year-old Cezary did not know that this acquaintance would turn his life in a completely new and unexpected direction.

Aurel Serafinczan

Aurel Serafinczan was a 30-year-old Romanian who, like many others, was sent to work in the mines near Ukhta. Before the exile, he lived with his wife in Chernivtsi, a city absorbed, along with the Romanian regions of Bukovina and Bessarabia, by the Soviet Union. At that time, it was a Ukrainian city lying near the Moldavian border. His father, Mikolaj ("me-KOH-li") Serafinczan, was a well-respected Pentecostal pastor and activist in those parts. Several times he was arrested and served sentences in various prisons and labor camps for pastoral work. When Aurel was in the camp in Komi, his father was held in Irkutsk (Siberia) at the same time.

Aurel's father was arrested and sentenced to work in the labor camps in 1948, together with other Evangelical pastors and preachers. Aurel and a close friend, Wasyl ("VA-sil"), decided to take over the ministry of his imprisoned father. They took care of the believers, led services, and tirelessly preached. Aurel did well at this because he was known as a good and recognized preacher from his youth. He also received from God the gift of prophecy, which began manifesting quite early. The Holy Spirit spoke through him on several occasions with incredible precision. The prophecies that he spoke were often fulfilled in an unusual manner. Therefore, he was quickly recognized in his area as a prophet.

One day as he prayed, he heard of the voice of the Holy Spirit say, "Prepare, because they will take you to another place. There, where I will send you, I have people."

Aurel immediately understood what God wanted to tell him. He judged that these words, spoken by the Holy Spirit, meant that he would certainly be arrested, convicted, and sent to a hard labor camp because the Gospel needed to be preached there and the believers needed pastoral care.

It was an exceptional moment and unique meeting with God which he defined as his call to ministry. He understood in his spirit that God had selected a place in which there were, or would be, people ordained by Him for salvation. God only needed a dedicated and loving person who would agree to reach them with the Good News, take care of them, and help them with spiritual development.

When Aurel finished talking with God, he knew his destiny was sealed. He said goodbye to his loved ones and packed a bundle of clothes, biscuits, and bread. He was ready!

The next night, his house resounded with the pounding of fists on the door. Aurel's eyes widened. It's time!

One of the KGB officers told him, "We came for you!"

To which he calmly replied, "I know that you came for me. I'm ready. I'm packed."

"What do you mean that you are ready?" the KGB officer asked suspiciously. "Who tipped you about the planned arrest?"

"It was not a man who told me but God, who sees everything!"

He was cuffed and taken into custody.

He was tried with his friend Wasyl and three other Pentecostal activists from his area. At the end of the trial, which was held behind closed doors, the prosecutor gave a fiery speech:

"You are a remnant of a bygone era!" he thundered. "You're a disgrace to the Soviet nation! You are agents of fascism! But we will destroy you! We will squash you like lice! We'll rip you out like weeds! I assure you that a time is coming when we'll make total order with you, and we will cleanse this nation of all that is anti-Soviet! We'll make order with this entire religious ignorance!"

After the accusing speech of the prosecutor, each of the defendants was given the opportunity for a last word. When it was Aurel's turn, he said:

"We are not a remnant of a bygone era. We are believers." He stopped for a moment and looked at the judge and prosecutor. "One thing is certain, we are certainly not fascists! It is you who are. Just as they destroyed and killed innocent people, so you also are engaged in these practices. What makes you different from the fascists and your labor camps different from the German concentration camps? You judge us today, and you know that we have not committed any crime against our nation. All of our guilt lies in the fact that we believe in God and proclaim His Word. You judge us for our faith and, in your hypocrisy, you do not even want to admit it."

The prosecutor arose with his face frozen in anger. "Your Honor," he said with a forced calmness. "I request that Aurel Serafinczan be sentenced to 25 years in correctional labor in the camps for anti-Soviet propaganda."

The judge raised his hammer, looked Aurel deeply in eyes, and said, "Aurel Serafinczan, based on Article 54 of the Ukrainian code, points 10 and 11, I sentence you to 25 years of correctional labor for anti-Soviet propaganda."

So on this day, Aurel received a sentence of 25 years in prison, and the rest of his companions received 10 years each. (In the 1940s and 1950s in Chernivtsi, as well as in the entire district, many pastors and preachers were arrested for the same reason. All of them received 10-year prison sentences based on Article 51. The only exception was Aurel, who became famous in the area for the fact that he received a sentence of 25 years!)

After the trial, Aurel was deported north to Komi ASSR. First, he was sent to the labor camps in the city of Ukhta where, with other convicts, he worked in a local factory where gas was processed into soot. From this soot, rubber tires were produced.

Later, he was sent to work extracting oil. At this unexpected place in his life's journey stood Cezary, who trained him for the job as a mine foreman. It was in this capacity that Aurel worked his next years in prison.

Aurel left behind in Chernivtsi a beautiful wife, Wasylisa ("Vah-sih-LEE-sa"), whom he loved with a passionate and pure love. His arrest and exile proved to be tragic for their marriage. After sending him deep into the Soviet Union, state agents worked on Wasylisa to leave him. They told her that the marriage had no chance because her husband would surely not return from exile. And if he did come back, he'd be a wreck.

They often threatened this defenseless woman, left in the face of life's tragedy, doing everything they could do to hinder her life. Among other things, they prevented her from finding any work. They also mentioned the stigma of her being married to a man convicted of Article 54 for anti-Soviet propaganda. At that time in the Soviet Union, this brought terrible shame to the family that closed the door to all possibilities. There was nothing worse than being an "anti-Soviet."

Wasylisa submitted to their pressure and divorced Aurel *in absentia*, and then later she married another man. Thus, Aurel lost his wife. He learned about it from the official letter that came to the camp where he was serving his sentence.

While working underground in the oil mine, the Holy Spirit again spoke to him: "I have brought you here. Here you should preach the Word of God because there are people here whom I have ordained for salvation."

From this experience, he understood that he had reached the place where he should start a church. Therefore, he had an even greater zeal for prayer and preaching the Gospel to win souls, in accordance with the message from the Holy Spirit. It turned out to be a difficult challenge. Some men Aurel won after several months. Others he persistently fought for over several years. And there were also people *not* won for Christ.

Something strange is happening with Cezary

Working together daily, Aurel and Cezary spent much time together talking about various topics. At last, Aurel asked Cezary a question: "How many years did you get?"

"Twenty-five years," he heard in response.

"Me, too! What are you in for?" he asked.

"For the Home Army," said Cezary. And he told Aurel the whole story about hiding weapons and ammunition, about later contact with the partisans, his arrest, and sentence. When he finished, he asked, "And what are you in for?"

"For God!" said Aurel with a firm voice and without hesitation.

"For God? How's that?" Cezary asked with surprise. "How can you be here because of God?"

"They imprisoned me because of faith in God and obedience to Him," said Aurel. "God spoke to me through the Holy Bible: 'I was naked and you clothed Me; I was sick and you visited Me; I was in prison, and you came to Me.' I tried to fulfill this Word. I did not commit any crime. It was God who wanted me to be sent to this camp and care for those who belong to Him. I was obedient to Him, and here I am to serve my Lord."

The story made a great impression on Cezary. "You are here for God?" he asked thoughtfully.

"Yes," nodded Aurel.

"I am a sinner because I'm here for the Home Army."

Later Aurel began to tell Cezary about God and the Word of God, urging him with his whole heart to read the Holy Bible. He said, "Cezary, read this book and your life will be transformed. It was written by inspiration of the Holy Spirit, and God speaks through it today."

In the beginning, Cezary was very reluctant to talk to Aurel about God and faith. He said, "I got *my* way, you got yours."

But Aurel was an above-average person. He was highly respected by his fellow inmates, and his lifestyle stirred more interest for Cezary. It came to the point that he could no longer ignore Aurel's words. If someone who lived everyday as Aurel did said something, his words had meaning. They could not be ignored. Cezary began to read pages of the New Testament that Aurel lent him. The Word of God very quickly spoke to him and moved this hard, young man to the depths.

Aurel told him: "Cezary, I like you very much. But despite the fact that you are a religious person, you are also a sinner and need God's transformation. You should start to pray, and when you spend time with God, He will begin to change your life. You will become someone completely new, and you will find in God extraordinary joy that I myself found."

Combined with prayer and discussions with other believers, studying the Word of God began having an important impact on Cezary.

As a result of fervent prayer and Aurel's dedicated missionary work, a total of 14 men were converted in this labor camp. Joining them was an earlier converted Baptist. In 1953, they formed an illegal community that operated underground. In order not to be detected, they met with different frequencies, at different times of the day, and in different places. Usually they met in barracks that were empty at any given time. Aurel called the believers his "sheaves," saying that they were the harvest that God gave him.

At some point in these illegal meetings, they invited Cezary, and he began to regularly participate in them. He quickly noted that something strange started to happen to him. He began to experience things that he did not understand, although he knew that they were very important. He loved cigarettes and smoked two packs a day; now, suddenly, he began to feel great anxiety every time he wanted to reach for a cigarette. Then one of the believers, the Baptist and one experienced in the Faith, realized that God had begun to work in Cezary's heart.

"Brother Cezary," he began with a serious voice, "the Holy Spirit is working on you. You should, therefore, prepare for His work. You need to know that we do not smoke cigarettes. Christ frees us from all addictions, and we can *live* in freedom. So, I advise you to say 'goodbye' to this habit. In our group, believers do not smoke!" Cezary stopped smoking, though he had loved cigarettes and never even thought about parting with his favorite addiction.

When in humility he met God, he also started to experience increasingly more joy, which filled his heart in an unusual way. The other believers quickly noticed that he had stopped cursing (earlier, he cursed all the time). They were certain that God had started His work in Cezary's life. They came to him, and one of them said solemnly, "Brother, we see that the Holy Spirit works in you, and Christ the Lord wants you to entrust Him with your whole life. We can see that you are starting to live differently than people who do not know God. Christ Himself is knocking at the door to your heart and encourages you to entrust Him with your life."

Cezary's conversion was a process; but, in the end, he dedicated his life to the Lord Jesus and experienced incredible joy. He walked in full happiness and satisfaction, which spurted in streams from the inside. He wanted to go to everyone and hug and kiss them! He even started to go in the direction of the guards, but his co-prisoners stopped him in time! "Kiewra, have you gone insane? You want to kiss the guards? After all, they'll shoot you on the spot! Stop, you fool! Do you want to end your life?"

Cezary's joy was so great that finally, to the surprise of the other prisoners, he confessed, "This labor camp is like paradise for me! Christ the Lord has given me incredible peace and joy. I can leave here. I can stay here and even die! It does not matter to me. I know that I am saved and, when I die, I will go to heaven. That is the most important thing! Everything else now is of little value!"

Christ the Lord became his life, and Cezary decided to serve Him until Jesus' second coming or his own death.

Brothers from Komi ASSR

The believers somehow managed to get the entire Holy Bible smuggled into the labor camp. It was cut into three parts, and each of them was beautifully covered. The Old Testament was divided into two, and the third part was the New Testament. Men secretly passed to each other various parts of the Bible, which was the most precious thing in the barren camp. Fragments circulated from one to another. They were constantly being read by prisoners hungry for God.

At times of joint secret meetings, the brothers discussed various fragments of the Holy Bible. They discussed how they should behave as believers and prevailed in joint prayers. In addition to this, Aurel, who was very sensitive to the Holy Spirit and gifted by Him, prophesied. They thoroughly analyzed each spoken word.

In this small underground church, the Holy Spirit, His guidance, and the prophetic word were very important. Aurel often "spoke in tongues" and then interpreted what God wanted to say to this small community. None of them knew theology. They did not know about *glossolalia*, meaning speaking and praying by the inspiration of the Holy Spirit. However, as a result of their personal reading of the Word, they were aware that these are gifts of the Comforter. They received them with all due seriousness.

One day the Holy Spirit said to them, "A roaring lion is circling around you and is looking to devour you. Do not worry. I will spare you, and I will reveal him to you."

It turned out that, at that time, one of the guards was hunting them and circled the barrack several times where they were meeting. One day, he came inside during prayer and caught them in the act.

The surprised men stopped praying, and he sternly ordered them to walk toward the camp headquarters. They walked humbly behind him, not knowing what this unexpected situation might lead to. The guard was planning to hand them over to the camp's authorities. Mindful, however, of the prophetic word of the Lord, one by one they broke off from the group and hid in their barracks. Finally, the guard turned around and was surprised to see that no one was following him. For some reason, he did not search for them.

In the barracks, one of the prisoners asked, "Is he a fool? He was lurking and lurking to capture you in prayer but, in the end, he let you all get away! It does not make sense!"

However, the Christians knew perfectly well that God Himself, in a wonderful way, saved them from the hand of the enemy. So they told their fellow prisoners about what actually had occurred that evening.

"When we prayed, the Lord Himself spoke and said that He saw our enemy, that he will turn against us but he will not do anything because God will save us from his clutches."

Thanks to Aurel's prophetic sensitivity, they were saved several times. Whenever he sensed coming danger, Aurel simply interrupted the meeting, saying, "God has revealed to me that the guards will be here soon. We need to escape at once!"

The other camp prisoners never betrayed them, and their guards never seized them because God watched over them!

Another time when they gathered, the Holy Spirit spoke through Aurel: "One of you has sticky hands." Immediately, they all began to carefully look at their hands which turned out to be clean. To this Aurel said, "It's not about whether your hands are literally dirty or clean. One of you took something, and now God is revealing it."

At that, one of the brothers arose and said, "Brother Aurel, God is indicating me! I am working in the warehouse, and I took a work coat. I didn't tell the warehouse foreman. You know it's a harsh winter!" To this Aurel replied, "I know. It is like you stole it. The Lord considered your act to be unclean. You must go to that man and tell him what you did."

On the second day, he obediently went to the warehouse foreman. "Listen, I took a work coat for myself." "It's nothing," said the foreman. "You took for yourself, so you took for yourself!"

The believers who converted in the camp asked Aurel to baptize them in water. They wanted in this way to give a public testimony of their faith in Jesus Christ. But one day, Aurel said to them, "Brothers, do not ask me anymore about that. After all, you know that I am not an ordained pastor. I think that it would be inappropriate if I were to baptize you here. But soon our situation will change. When you leave here free, find some church where you live that has true servants of God and become a part of it. When this happens, tell how you met God here in the North. Then ask one of the pastors there to baptize you with the baptism of faith by immersion in water."

Polish territory after the Second World War
From Wikszniany through Orsha to Ukhta in the Komi ASSR was about 1500 miles

Sitting (from the left), Aurel and Cezary

On the back the note:

"Brothers from Komi ASRR, North, years 1953-1955

Andrew Mytych

3

From Siberia to Poland

In search of one's own

"Soon we'll leave here."

During a prayer meeting in the labor camp, God spoke through Aurel: "Soon I will liberate you, and you will leave here. You can prepare to return to your homes!"

Great joy descended, and hope filled the hearts of all those praying. They were convinced that the Americans would enter the Soviet Union and liberate all the prisoners in the labor camps, including them.

They started to share the good news with other prisoners. "Soon we'll leave here!" they exclaimed as they repeated these words of prophecy. "God has revealed to us that we can prepare to return to our homes!"

But other prisoners indicated that they were crazy! "What is the matter with you guys? Have you, at last, gone crazy? Your faith has completely messed up your senses! We will never leave here. We will be in the camps to the end. We will all die like dogs!"

One of the convicted pointed to the area behind the barbed-wire fence: "There, in that ground, under the snow, your bodies will lie!"

Reality in the labor camps was cruel. People forgot about morality, principles, and a feeling of dignity while trying to survive without hope. The convicts, detached from society, did not believe that they were able to out-live long sentences. Even if they did survive, they could not imagine that they would receive from the government permission to return to their homeland.

The Americans did not invade the Soviet Union and liberate the camps. But six months after Aurel spoke the prophecy, something happened that no one expected. According to the official statement made on March 5, 1953, Joseph Stalin, leader and dictator of the Soviet Union, died! Soon afterwards, large-scale political amnesty was announced, and thousands of prisoners were freed.

Aurel and Cezary left the camp along with the other brothers— all except for one. This man very much loved his family. He missed them and prayed daily, asking God for freedom because he very much desired to return to his family.

However, during one evening prayer meeting, Aurel spoke under the inspiration of the Holy Spirit: "Thus says the Lord, 'Your table is turned upside down.'" The believers interpreted this prophecy to mean, "From the family table you will no longer eat."

He was the only one of the 16 prison believers who did not leave, dying in the camp.

Great political thaw

The death of Joseph Stalin, dictator of the Union of Soviet Socialist Republics (USSR), caused genuine grief to millions of inhabitants of this huge country. A wave of mourning marches and rallies went through the entire nation. Thousands of people from different parts of the country went to Moscow to say goodbye to a man who, in life, had become a legend. Even those who were the victims of his brutal rule wept with sorrow for Stalin.

When news of Stalin's death reached the labor camp at "crude oil mine No. 2" in Ukhta, neither Cezary nor Aurel wept. In their hearts appeared the hope that something might change. Shortly, it turned out that the dream was not unfounded. A political thaw slowly took place.

The state structure was reorganized. On March 27, 1953, the Supreme Soviet (parliament) announced amnesty. Political prisoners who received sentences up to 5 years in prison were released; the others had their sentence reduced by half or even more. Cezary's case was reviewed on September 5, 1953, by the Military Tribunal Court of the Byelorussian District, and his judgment was shortened to 10 years. The repressive system was eased, but labor camps were not yet abandoned. So Cezary still remained a prisoner of the Gulag system.

In September of 1953, Nikita Khrushchev became the First Secretary of the Communist Party of the Soviet Union as well as Premier. He began to gradually introduce changes and reform in the country. These activities were relatively cautious because many people did not understand why the order established by Comrade Stalin and his structure of power should be changed. Khrushchev limited the cult of Stalin and also suppressed the perverse methods of governance.

During the final years of his sentence, Cezary worked in the mine which had particularly difficult conditions. For this reason, as mentioned earlier, each day of work resulted in three days being deducted from his sentence. Thanks to that, he worked a total of 6 years in the labor camp. In the end, he regained his freedom, and the camp "at oil mine camp No. 2" was closed. It was transformed into "free housing estate No. 2".

After obtaining his freedom, Cezary still worked by mining crude oil and waited for permission to be able to return home. During this period in the Soviet Union, people were not able to move freely within their own country. They had to first obtain permission. The migration of people was strictly regulated by the government.

Since Aurel was arrested earlier than Cezary, he was the first to obtain freedom and permission to return home. Before going back to Chernivtsi, he met with Cezary in the housing estate. "Don't keep me here any longer, Cezary! I very much desire to see my family and friends who remained in Bukovina. I want to see my father. I want to go back to my family!"

They warmly parted, thanked God for everything that they had experienced from Him, and Aurel took the train to his longed-for Bukovina.

In the late 1940s and 1950s, the Soviet authorities carried out research on the economic efficiency of the Gulag. It turned out that it was an economically inefficient institution which had to be maintained by the state. In addition, it failed to meet its primary goal—it did not re-educate prisoners. It was doubtful that many of those who left the barbed-wire camps left them as communists or even as better citizens. The Gulag had transformed into an inefficient company using slave labor. In 1957, the Gulag system was terminated.

Return to the family village

At the end of September 1956, Cezary was given the appropriate documents of release and, in a state of rapture, was able to leave Ukhta and return home. He had worked in the crude oil mine for 4 years. In total, he spent 6 years in exile in the harsh climate of Siberia, away from his home village. He sincerely thanked God for his survival even when many of his companions in suffering had died. On the return trip to Wikszniany, the train first went to Moscow where Cezary spent the entire day. He walked the streets of this beautiful and large city and also visited the Moscow zoo. Everything looked so much different here than in *Komi ASSR!* The city vibrated with life. In no way did it resemble the harsh scenery of Siberia! At night, he took the train to Minsk. From there, the next train to Juraciszki. Then, on foot and with a suitcase in his hand, he marched to Wikszniany.

When he approached the family home, his mother happened to be in the doorway with a basket in her hands. Shocked, she began to scream, "Cezary returned! Cezary returned! Cezary returned!"

The whole family was overcome with happiness, and great joy came upon the Kiewra house. Cezary's brothers immediately wanted to fill the cups with moonshine to celebrate his return. Cezary stopped them and calmly explained that he had returned from the North as a new man, reborn by God. They had no idea what he was talking about. However, they were extremely overjoyed by the fact that he was released from prison.

The villagers were also very pleased with his return. From the very beginning, they noticed the changes in Cezary, and it amazed them! Before his exile to the labor camps, Cezary organized village parties, was the life of the party, and a known ladies' man. Now his values were totally changed. In the Gulag, he had decided that he would serve God with his entire heart. In addition to this, the years spent in the Gulag left their mark on every man and transformed personalities. Cezar returned from Siberia as a serious and mature man.

He again took up tailoring because he was good at it. Throughout the year, he worked privately, sewing for his neighbors. He was also involved in the lives of believers living in the area. In Wikszniany lived the Janinka ("Yah-NEEN-kah") family whom he met with weekly to pray. On a regular basis, he also attended church services in Milki ("MEEL-kee"), a town about 12 miles away. Together with this family, they walked or rode bicycles there because in those times, cars were quite rare, especially in the countryside.

The church in Milki was founded by a Polish repatriate from the United States who, before the war, returned from America to start Pentecostal churches in his homeland. Most likely he was killed in March 1943 by German occupiers. His body was identified by the clothing during exhumation of a mass grave in Vileyka.

In October 1956, Cezary was baptized by immersion in the river. That month in autumn was very cold, but the strong need to give a public testimony of his faith in Christ and devoting his life to Him gave Cezary courage. The piercing cold was not a hindrance. And after his baptism, he told his story of conversion and shared the burning desire to serve God.

Journey to Poland

During and after the war, Nikodem, Cezary's father, had been sending letters from England to his wife Wiktoria, imploring her to move with their sons to Poland from where, in some way, he wanted to help them get to Great Britain. Having been a soldier in Anders' Army, he was aware that he would not be able to leave Great Britain to go to the Soviet Union to help his family emigrate. On the other hand, his family could not directly leave that country to go to England.

In the years 1944-1946, from the western parts of the Soviet Union where the Wikszniany village was located, there occurred the first repatriation of the Poles. To a large extent, they were displaced to the so-called Recovered Territories, a term used by the Republic of Poland that referred to land which belonged to pre-war Germany and that was returned to Poland after World War II. Wiktoria decided not to go to Poland because the fate of her husband Nikodem was just being settled abroad.

Soon, the possibility to go to Poland closed. It did not open again until 8 years later, in 1953. Persons who before September 17, 1939, were Polish citizens (as well as their spouses and children) could benefit from this possibility.

Nikodem's hope to be reunited with his family was not weakened by the years of forced separation. The second repatriation again gave his family a chance, but it turned out that leaving the communist Soviet Union was not as simple as it might appear for the Kiewra family.

Nikodem asked a friend, Marian Nizioł (MAHR-yan NEE-zhoow), then a resident of Nowa Huta ("NOH-vah HOO-tah"), to invite Wiktoria and the children to this city outside of Kraków ("KRAH-koof"). In 1957, Wiktoria twice applied for permission for repatriation to Poland, but each time the local officials rejected her applications. She was informed that she would not receive permission because her husband had served in Anders' Army and then settled in capitalist Great Britain. It was simultaneously suggested that if she sold to the state her home in Wikszniany, then her application might be granted.

The possibility to take advantage of the second repatriation gradually began to close, and the Kiewra family anxiously watched as their friends, neighbors, and relatives immigrated to Poland. They felt completely helpless and, in their hearts, they knew that their fate was already sealed. Only the loss of their house gave some sort of a chance to move to Poland and, later, the possibility to join Nikodem.

Their family home was a large, wooden building built by Nikodem on a brick foundation before World War II. The authorities wanted it for a primary school. Due to its size and good condition, it was suitable for this purpose. Finally, the Kiewra family came to the conclusion that it was better to trade their house for freedom than to be forever, to some extent, imprisoned in the USSR.

After thorough consideration of the matter, they sold the home to the authorities. As a result, they obtained permission to go to Poland. They decided to leave Wikszniany immediately after receiving the documents. Money from the sale of the house was used to buy a German "Diamant" bicycle, a motorcycle, and a gold watch.

On February 21, 1958, Wiktoria, her four sons, and her pregnant daughter-in-law Anna got onto the train heading to Poland. As luggage they had the bicycle, motorcycle, an old sewing machine of Cezary's, some clothes, and pots. This was everything they had to take out of the Soviet Union.

Together with other repatriates, they first arrived in a city in eastern Poland where people displaced from the Soviet East were segregated and sent deep into Poland. The Kiewras were then processed in accordance to the invitation to Nowa Huta, to Marian Nizioł, Nikodem's old friend. From this city, Nikodem intended to bring his family to Great Britain to be together again after many years of separation.

By the end of the 1950s, this socrealistic city (filled with art and architecture that promoted socialism and communism) did not suit the tastes of the Kiewra family. Also, Marian Nizioł had a small apartment. When the family had to sleep on the floor in the kitchen and another room on the first night, Adam, Cezary's brother, burst into tears. "Let's go to Lubań ("LOO-bahn"). I learned that in Lubań and Olszyna ("Ol-SHIH-nah"), they are settling our people from Wikszniany. Our people are there, so that is our place!"

They all agreed that he was right. After all, their place was where people from their villages were. They decided to travel to

Lubań, to the Recovered Territories. They got off at the Lubań railway station on February 28, 1958, and immediately reported to the authorities. They received a two-room apartment with a toilet in the yard. The entire Kiewra family—Wiktoria with four adult sons and her pregnant daughter-in-law—lived there.

Slowly, they started to build a new life. Anna found work at the post office and her husband Wiktor in construction. Janek became a mechanic with PKS (the state bus line), and Adam worked doing odd jobs. Wiktoria took care of the home while Cezary took up tailoring. Throughout 1958, he worked in Lubań at a private tailor shop whose owner was a master in his trade. Cezary learned how to sew for the needs of the urban population because, until this point in his life, he had sewed mainly for village residents in Belarus. Orders in his former village of Wikszniany and its surroundings were not complicated. They mainly consisted in sewing and repairing straight-cut clothes and furs. Cezary spoke of himself as a village tailor. But, in Lubań, he developed his skills, learning to sew coats and suits.

Wiktoria joins her husband

At last, in 1959, Wiktoria and her son Adam went to Nikodem in Great Britain. Polish immigrants, who after World War II settled on the Islands, were allowed to have their spouses and minor-aged children immigrate to them. By this time, all of Nikodem's sons were adults, so they were not entitled to the right of immigration. However, Wiktoria managed to take their youngest son to England. Nikodem made sure that Adam would not have to return to communist Poland.

What a meeting that was! In late August of 1939, 35-year-old Nikodem had left his home in Wikszniany, bidding farewell to Wiktoria and their four sons. He never thought that he would not see them for the next 20 years!

Throughout this entire time, Nikodem waited to be reunited with his family. He sent them letters and packages from England and patiently waited.

Cezary and the other 2 brothers did not emigrate from communist Poland, although it was a different country than in the first phase of Stalinist oppression.

The search for the brothers in Christ

After settling in Poland, Cezary made a firm decision that he would look for other Pentecostals in order to join people who were as devoted to God as he was. This was not so easy. Where should he look for them? In Lubań, he did not find Pentecostals. So, he regularly rode his bike to the nearby areas to ask about people who were like-minded believers. He went to many towns and villages, but no one knew of any such people living nearby. In the autumn of 1958, after much investigation, Cezary's search paid off.

In one city, he met a man who, after listening carefully, said, "I heard that Pentecostals are in Lwówek Śląski ("Luh-VOO-vek SHLOHN-skee"). I was told that a group of about 30 people gather there. Go to that town and certainly you'll find the people you are looking for."

Overjoyed, Cezary rode his bike to Lwówek Śląski the following Sunday. There he stopped a gentleman and asked, "Sir, do you know of any people who are practicing believers?"

The man turned on his heels, pointed to the building opposite and said, "Right here, in the pickling plant, work the Ciechanowski ("Cheh-ha-NOHF-skee") sisters. Go to these maidens and ask them."

"And who are they?" added Cezary. "Are they Pentecostal?"

"I don't know," answered the passer-by. "I know only that these people bathe."

"They bathe?" Cezary asked with amazement. "What do you mean, they bathe?"

"Well, they dip into the river."

"Oh," smiled Cezary. "You probably mean that they get baptized in the river."

"Sir, I have no idea what they get or do in that river. I don't know. You'd better go and talk with the sisters."

Cezary took a few brisk steps in the direction of the plant's gate, stopped in front of the entrance, trying to get a look at the girls. It just so happened that on that day, cabbage was brought which urgently needed to be unloaded. The sisters were asked to help. Cezary got there during lunch break, so the girls were sitting in the yard.

They saw him and curiously approached the gate. Cezary asked, "Are you the Ciechanowski sisters?"

"Yes," they replied in unison.

"Are you Pentecostals?"

"Yes, we are," they replied, staring curiously at his face.

"I am your brother in Christ," he said solemnly. "I am also Pentecostal!"

At that, one of the sisters pointed to a building across the street and said, "Brother, Pentecostals live in half of the house which you see there. Today there will be a prayer meeting in that place, and I think, Brother, that you should remain with us."

Cezary accepted their invitation with joy. He was invited inside by the girls' father who was already a believer. In the evening, they all went together to the prayer meeting.

At the request of the pastor of the church in Lwówek, Cezary introduced himself and told his story. He talked about how God found him in the far North, and then how he participated in the life of believers in Belarus. After hearing his story, the whole group greeted him warmly.

Cezary in front of the mine on the first day of freedom, 1956

Aurel (on the left) and Cezary, now free;

suits made by Cezary

Cezary's documents

allowing him to

return home

Church in Milki, 1939

**Cezary (2nd from the right) in Nowogrodek
after a church service, 1957**

Kiewra family repatriation route to the Regained Territories, winter 1958

Andrew Mytych

4

Finding Rebecca

Love, matrimony, and other difficulties

Marriage to Łucja

Cezary began to regularly ride his bike to the church in Lwówek Śląski. He had a strong conviction that Christ the Lord had also brought him to this fellowship in order to give him a wife. In time, he realized that deep feelings for Łucja ("WOOTS-yah") Ciechanowska were born in his heart. Both Ciechanowska sisters were ready for marriage, but he gave his love to Łucja.

During this time, engagement in the Lwówek Śląski church was taken very seriously. Repatriated believers who brought their traditions and sense of morality from churches in the East established a lot of requirements and discipline in this matter. It was unthinkable for a strong Pentecostal believer to date "some" girl or kiss her. There were cases of violations of these rigid rules, but Cezary decided to maintain restraint and live in fear of God. He believed that premarital purity is the absolute norm and will of God.

Early in the spring of 1959, he had a serious talk with the pastor to tell him about his feelings for Łucja and his specific intentions toward her.

"Hmm," mused the pastor. "It may be even better," he finally said. Then he laughed good-naturedly and added, "I see, Cezary, that you have found your *Rebecca*! Ok, I will go to the Ciechanowskis and talk with them."

When the Ciechanowskis agreed to the wedding, Cezary ceremonially proposed to Łucja on March 8, 1959, and she accepted the marriage proposal and said, "I do." She liked Cezary's mature dedication to God.

On March 21, 1959, after agreeing on the details and completion of all the formalities, they had a civil ceremony in Lwówek. After the ceremony in city hall, they ate a ceremonial dinner. Then Cezary rode back to Lubań on his bike! Pentecostals believed that the marriage at city hall only had an administrative nature. It was not fully sanctioned because it was not concluded before God. In order to avoid the sin of fornication, the wedding night had to wait until the church ceremony. Eight days later, on March 29, 1959, Cezary and Łucja were married at the Pentecostal Church in Lwówek Śląski.

Łucja dreamed about arriving at the church in a taxi. However, in Lwówek Śląski, there was only one taxi and, unfortunately, that day it suddenly "disappeared." The young couple had no choice. Together, with her parents and the guests, they marched in joyful step to the church.

Cezary kissed his wife for the first time on the church wedding day. They believed that keeping themselves pure brings glory to God and is necessary to ensure that God will bless their marriage in the future.

The wedding reception was held in the Ciechanowskis' apartment which, on that special day, held about 70 people—family, neighbors, Lwówek Śląski church members, and believing youth from Legnica ("Leg-NEETS-ah"), the pastor's home city about 40 miles away. In those times, guests did not give gifts to newlyweds. The believers simply sang, joyfully ate the wedding meal, and left. Those who came from far away stayed the night.

When the reception was over, it was time for the long-awaited wedding night! The newlyweds were glad that they had kept their purity for that special night as it became a strong foundation for their future good and long-lasting marriage.

Sometime later, the young married couple set off on their honeymoon. They got on their bicycles and went on a romantic "honeymoon cycling trip." First, they rode to Gryfów Śląski ("GRIH-foof SHLOHN-skee") where they spent the entire day. They visited Łucja's brother and, in the evening, went to Lubań. This was an opportunity for Łucja to meet Cezary's family. From Lubań, they went for 3 days to the countryside of Świecie ("SVYEH-cheh") where a family of believers lived. The home was run by a lame man named Zajko ("ZI-koh"). He had invited them, and joyfully gave the loving couple one of the rooms in his cottage.

Fate of the Ciechanowski family

Łucja Ciechanowska was born in 1937 in Zdolbuniv ("zdohl-BOO-neef") near Rivne ("REEV-neh"), which is part of Ukraine today. Her parents had different origins. Her father, Józef ("YOU-sef") Ciechanowski, was a Pole. Early orphaned, he had to work to earn a living. He was illiterate. Her mother, Olga, was German.

When the Polish-Ukrainian conflicts began in 1940s, and in view of Olga's ethnic origin, the immediate family managed to escape to the Third Reich. However, during the time of the nationalistic slaughter of the Polish civilian population living in Ukraine, Ukrainians from the UPA (the Ukrainian Insurgent Army) killed Olga's sister in a cruel manner, cutting her body in two. Such cruelties were not separate incidents but a frequent practice.

When the family arrived in the Reich, they were first in a transitional camp where conditions were difficult and where several families were placed in each room. From there, the Ciechanowskis were transferred to Leipzig, Germany, where they received a 2-bedroom apartment on the ground floor with a toilet in the corridor. For the first year, Józef worked in a factory and then also moonlighted doing odd jobs when he got the chance. Olga did not work. She reared the children, most of whom, unfortunately, died. In total, she gave birth to 7 children, but only Łucja and Teresa, who was 2 years younger, survived. In June 1945, Olga Ciechanowska died at the age of 39 while trying to give birth.

Józef was left alone with two young daughters. After much thought, he decided to move to Poland in 1946. Although many Poles (who for various reasons then lived in Germany) immigrated to the United States, Józef wanted to rear his daughters in their homeland.

He got on a freight train with his daughters and headed to Poland. They took food, a few bundles of clothes, and 3 mattresses. This was all they had when they got off in what is now called Zgorzelec ("zgoh-ZHEH-lets"), at that time called Gorlitz. Less than a year before, it was an entirely German town. Now, divided by the Nysa River, it became a border town. In Zgorzelec, the Ciechanowski family took over an apartment in a large and beautiful former German house.

Józef was not yet working anywhere, but he had an extremely-developed sense for business. He went to the villages, bought various products from the farmers, and then sold them at markets in nearby cities—most often the market in Lubań. He sold young bulls, milk, eggs, and such goods. He would rent a wagon, pack it with agricultural products, load his daughters onto the wagon, and head for the market. This is how he earned money to support his family. His ingenuity and practical approach allowed them to survive the difficult post-war period. In a shed, he also kept a goat that the girls fed. The animal didn't take up much space, it could graze anywhere, and it gave the family milk. (During this period, many families raised goats.)

In the beginning of 1947, the faucet broke in the apartment, and Józef earnestly began looking for a plumber because he didn't know how to fix it himself. Finally, after a long search, he approached a young man on the street. "Do you know anything about plumbing? My faucet broke."

The boy grinned from ear to ear and said in German, "Yes, I know about plumbing. I *am* a plumber!"

"Well, Boy, come with me. You will save me!"

When the faucet was repaired, Józef asked with interest, "What's your name, Son?"

"Helmut," the boy replied hesitantly.

"Tell me, Helmut, do you live alone?"

"No," he said. "I live with my mother. My father is dead."

"Listen, maybe your mama can come to us sometime. I have two small girls to rear who are without their mother because my German wife died. One of my daughters is 6 years old and the other is 8. Maybe your mother could do some washing or cook something sometime. I really need help."

To this the boy replied, "All right. I will tell her, and she will come."

Then Józef gave him some money and said goodbye.

The day after the visit of the young plumber, a German woman, Emmie, stood at the family's door. She willingly, and with great commitment, helped in the Ciechanowski apartment. For her work in the home, Józef gave her food—butter, eggs, and milk.

Emmie was then 36 years old, and her husband had died in Russia fighting on the Eastern Front. She was born and reared in East Prussia (part of the then-German state of Prussia), in areas that today belong to Russia. As the Red Army advanced toward Berlin, Emmie and her son Helmut were put on a ship headed for Germany. Escape from the approaching Soviet Army was often a very horrific experience! The worst of the tragedies was seeing children thrown from the shore to departing refugee ships that were under full Soviet attack by gunfire. Many of the children fell into the sea and drowned. In spite of the enormous difficulties, Emmie and her teenage son survived the trip to Germany. In Leipzig, a family took them in and settled them in the basement.

After World War II, when the situation somewhat stabilized, Emmie and Helmut packed all of their property onto 2 bikes and set off. They planned to travel through Poland to their hometown in former East Prussia. In Zgorzelec, on the Polish side, the border guards took all they had. When she stood there like a pillar of salt, one of the Poles said, "Now you can go. Get out of here! *Schnell!*"

They were completely confused and overwhelmed by the situation, but they managed to find an abandoned apartment in the border city. They did not know what happened to the previous residents of the apartment who had left their furniture, dishes, and clothes. Because Emmie's son was a good plumber, he repaired things in different places and was able to earn a living. This is how they survived day to day.

Later, thanks to her son, Emmie happened upon the home of Józef Ciechanowski and his daughters, and hope for a better life shown brighter. In time, Józef and Emmie fell in love with each other and wanted to get married. But this was impossible because Germans were being caught, packed into freight wagons, and exported to Germany in mass.

Józef hid Emmie on a farm in a village near Zgorzelec and saved her from forced deportation to Germany. (Many Germans were deported from Zgorzelec after they were robbed of everything they had.) The Ciechanowski sisters often played near the railway station and so sometimes saw how people's things were taken just before being put into the wagons. Besides, a deported German could only have 44 pounds of baggage.

After some time, the girls, who fluently spoke German, became friends with two older German women. One day the women invited the sisters to their apartment. They opened the cabinets one by one and said, "Look! Poles took everything we had! They looted everything! We only have one pot!"

They were robbed of everything, even clothes, condemning the vulnerable women to hunger. The girls, touched by this personal disaster, brought them bread with butter every day on their way to school. The girls were supposed to eat it themselves during class breaks!

When the sisters went to the courtyard to play, they were often beaten and had stones or bottles thrown at them by the Polish children. Because they spoke German and were cared for by a German woman, their peers saw them as Germans and treacherously took revenge on them. After all, half of their blood was German, since their mother was native German. One time the children were so brutal in beating Łucja that a bone protruded out of her elbow.

The Ciechanowskis spent only 2 years in Zgorzelec. Over them lived an intelligent Polish family. One of their sons worked in the magistrate's office, and the other son worked in another office. Because the house where they lived was beautiful, they were vulnerable to the tense times. One day in the spring of 1948, the Ciechanowskis received an official letter which ordered them to leave Zgorzelec within the next 24 hours and to a distance at least 20 miles away. Not having any choice, Józef rented a truck and packed the mattresses, chairs, clothing, food, and the goat as well as Emmie, her son Helmut, and his two daughters. Nothing more would fit, so the rest of their belongings had to stay in Zgorzelec.

They arrived in Lwówek Śląski and unpacked everything they had right onto the street. And the truck left. They looked around and saw a tenement building in which there was an empty apartment on the second floor. Without thinking too long, they carried all their things there. They threw the mattresses on the floor and put the chairs next to them. After looking over all their belongings, a neighbor who lived below muttered under her breath, "I'll give you one table. I have too many."

In time, they were able to buy two used, German metal beds. However, they were not to live here long. They moved to another house where they occupied the first floor while the goat lived in the laundry room.

Emmie rarely left the house. Being German, she was afraid of the Poles who shot at her several times with air rifles from the building across the street. Fortunately, they always missed.

Soon, Emmie's son got a job in construction as a plumber. Over time, he needed an assistant, so he began to take Józef with him. This allowed Józef to learn plumbing and successfully work in this profession.

The Ciechanowskis' road to God

Emmie had participated for 5 years in a Christian community in Eastern Prussia, singing in the choir and playing the mandolin. When the war broke out, she no longer practiced her faith. And then she married Józef, who was Catholic. The whole time, however, she read the Bible in German. In general, she was an extremely intelligent and well-read woman.

The girls daily grazed the goat in the ruins of homes destroyed during the war. One day, two women came to them who were Pentecostals and who had been repatriated from the Eastern Borderlands. They found out that Józef Ciechanowski was connected to a German woman, so they assumed that she was probably a Protestant. They said to the girls, "Listen, we are believers. We gather for prayer meetings and study the Bible. Maybe you'll come to such a meeting and see what our services look like?"

"Maybe one day we will come," said Łucja uncertainly.

"We would also like to talk to your mom," said one of the women.

"But how?" asked Łucja. "Do you speak German? Our mother is German and does not know Polish. At home, we only talk with her in German. Besides, she is afraid of Poles. Whenever she is by herself, she locks the door and doesn't let anyone in."

"It's not a problem. We'll come when you will be at home with your mom, and you can help us communicate. You'll translate our conversations."

Later, both women went to visit Emmie. They shared about the Word of God and talked about the Pentecostal Church in Lwówek Śląski. They also invited her to the meetings, and finally Emmie decided to go there with her husband and children. She started to regularly participate in the meetings with her daughters although, in the beginning, Józef was very against it. He would say, "We have the Catholic church here. Come to our church. Why would you go to these people?"

There was something, though, that drew Emmie and her daughters to the Pentecostal meetings.

In 1953, the girls converted and received from the believers a Bible which they started to read. After reading it for some time, they realized that the Bible is true and that they should fully entrust their lives to the Lord Jesus. The pastor also had a great influence on the girls' conversion. In order to return to Legnica (where he lived at the time) after the meetings in Lwówek, he first had to walk 1.2 miles to the railway station. He was escorted by a swarm of kids and teenagers, and he taught the Gospel and the Word of God along the way. He told them Bible stories, joked, asked various riddles, and taught them practical things related to the Christian life. It was a kind of Sunday School class, and the children remembered them all their lives. Among those who escorted the pastor were Łucja and Teresa.

In 1954, Emmie, without the knowledge of her husband, asked to be baptized in accordance with the Evangelical conviction that personal faith is its condition. She was baptized with one other woman whose husband had also been against his wife's conversion. They were baptized in the Bóbr River that ran through Lwówek. One year later, 18-year-old Łucja, also without the knowledge of her father, was baptized. She joined other new converts for a baptism organized by the Pentecostal Church in Wrocław ("VROHTS-waf"), a large city approximately 100 miles from Lwówek.

In 1956, Teresa was baptized in that river, too. Every year, from surrounding churches, people went there and stood for Jesus through the visible act of immersion in water and gave their lives fully to Him. Teresa was baptized with a large group that included her future husband, Stefan Kuśnierz ("KOOSH-nyezh"). He would later become pastor of the church in Lwówek Śląski. Teresa did not hide her baptism from her father who was surprised to see her dressed in white.

"What is happening, Dear? Why are you dressed in white?"

"I'm going to be baptized, Daddy," she replied. Józef did not respond then. He loved his daughters very much. They were the apple of his eye.

The man who defended orthodoxy with an ax

Józef Ciechanowski could not accept his wife's conversion, but the real blow was his daughters' conversions. He had a great grudge towards his wife Emmie because he considered himself a fervent Catholic and all other believers as wanderers from the Faith. When his wife and daughters talked at home about God, the Bible, or the Pentecostal Church, he went crazy!

He was very against the Pentecostals because he believed that they had stolen his children from him. When the pastor of the church with another young man wanted to visit him and talk, he put an ax on the threshold and shouted to his wife, "They had better not come in here because I'll chop them up! I swear I'll chop them into pieces on the spot!"

However, Emmie and the girls regularly went to church meetings twice a week. They knew that Józef's behavior was caused by a lack of understanding and a great love for his family. He feared for his wife and daughters. Therefore, he tried to protect them anyway he could from that which he did not understand and, as a Catholic, what he condemned.

The women respected Józef; but, at the same time, they felt an increasingly greater love toward Christ and the Bible. They also desired baptism in the Holy Spirit, which the Pentecostals talked about often. They earnestly asked God to pour out His Spirit on them. Finally, Teresa, even before her baptism of faith, started to speak in other languages in her home. The Holy Spirit came upon her in such a powerful way that she could not stop praying in tongues the entire night, practicing one of the gifts of the Spirit!

Józef was terrified. He wanted to call an ambulance!

"What have you done to her?" he bitterly asked his wife and Łucja. "What happened to her that you can't talk normally with her now? What language is that anyway that she is speaking? Did something get messed up in her head and she is going to babble like this all the time?"

"Nothing happened to her," Emmie replied calmly. "God gave her grace. The Holy Spirit came upon her, and she is speaking in other languages which are from God."

"You're talking nonsense, Woman!" Józef angrily gasped. "You have gone crazy and dragged my beloved daughter into your insanity!"

❧ ❧ ❧ ❧ ❧

He often resentfully complained to his colleague at work. "They stole my wonderful children. Do you understand? They stole my children!"

His colleague, like Józef, was an ardent Catholic. He understood his pain and helped in the fight against Pentecostal piety anyway he could. He encouraged Józef not to give up and to fight for his family.

With time, love for his family prevailed, and Józef calmed down. His wife and daughters regularly went to the church in Lwówek, so in order to be near his beloved women, Józef began to accompany them. And one day, he believed! On this particular Sunday, he experienced an extraordinary meeting with God that opened his eyes to the Gospel and gave him understanding.

On Monday, he went to work, having decided that he would not keep his "new birth" a secret only for himself. He felt that he must share the Good News with all of his colleagues and, in particular, with the friend who helped him in the fight *against* the Pentecostals.

"Friends, I converted," he said in brief.

"What did you do?" asked a co-worker, thinking that he misheard.

"I accepted Christ as my Lord and Savior," he said.

Then the former friend came up to him and, with all his might, punched him on the right side of his face! "You heretic!" he angrily growled.

When Józef shook off the punch, he turned his other cheek to him, saying, "If yes, then I turn the other cheek. Beat me!"

"Yes? You believed? Look how he became a believer all of a sudden," he laughed mockingly. "Well, here you go, you heretic!" and, with all his strength, punched Józef on the left cheek.

The insults and unpleasant words spoken by Józef's colleagues did not discourage him. He had experienced a meeting with God, and he knew Who he could trust. God brought to his life extraordinary joy and peace, and he regularly told colleagues from work about Christ, the Bible, and church. The men laughed at him and made fun of him, but he didn't take it to heart. He remembered perfectly well that he, too, had not understood the faith of his wife and daughters and what they experienced with God.

Shortly after his conversion, he experienced a painful but enlightening escapade that helped him to daily walk with Christ in a radical way. While still a Catholic, he had the custom after Sunday mass of going to the local bar for a beer. One Sunday, soon after his conversion, he concluded that one beer wouldn't hurt anyone. So, after the church service, he went to the bar. News of how he was going to another church had already gone around Lwówek Śląski.

"One beer," he said to the bartender.

"What? Beer?" the bartender asked, raising his voice. "I'll give you a beer, you heretic!"

The bartender then quickly leaned over the counter and before Józef had any idea of what was about to happen, he got punched in the face so hard by the bartender that his back hit the floor and his legs went over his head!

"After all, you heretics don't drink," said the barman in a somewhat calmer voice. "So what are you doing, Ciechanowski, in my bar?"

He grabbed Józef by the collar and threw him out. Bidding farewell, the bartender said, "I don't want to see you anymore in my bar!"

Some laughed at the Pentecostals, but everyone knew that to be one meant leading a decent life. It was expected that they would be honest, that no man would cheat on his wife, and that they wouldn't smoke or drink. Therefore, it was not acceptable for a *real* Pentecostal to walk into a bar for a beer.

Józef Ciechanowski converted with all his heart, and this was an extremely deep experience for him. He also decided to enter into a covenant with God through the baptism of faith.

In order to perform a baptism in these communistic times, a church pastor had to submit a special request to the local authorities which described the event in detail. The pastor of the Lwówek church submitted such a letter and received permission, but the place of the ceremony was strictly defined by the officials. However, the Bóbr River was overflowing, and he did not know what to do. After some thought, he decided that the baptism should be performed in a different place. He chose the nearby Płóczka ("PWOOCH-ka") River, which was also overflowing, but the water was relatively calm. So, Józef was baptized in this place on July 13, 1958.

Because the place of the baptism was changed, the pastor had a lot of problems. The matter was even brought to the prosecutor's office.

Unexpected answer to prayer

One of the reasons why Józef did not initially approve of his daughters' conversion was his fear—and care—for their future. He wanted them to find decent husbands and have a good life. However, much to his displeasure, they converted and began to earnestly serve God. Neither of them even wanted to hear about the cinema, theater, dances, and parties. He looked around the small (at that time) church in Lwówek Śląski and asked himself, "To whom will I give my daughters in marriage?" He didn't see any worthy candidates, and the young ladies did not worry too much about the matter of their marriages. They trusted God that, at the right time, He would place in their lives the right men.

At that time in the Pentecostal Church, young people prayed to God for the right partner, and the entire church prayed, too. Łucja had the desire for marriage in her heart, trusting God that He would answer her prayer at the right time.

Józef viewed this approach for seeking a spouse with great skepticism. He was terrified by what his eyes saw! Łucja was ready for marriage, but here was such "poverty"! Instead of looking for a husband, she was only focused on the Bible, Christ, and prayer. However, on one Sunday afternoon, a handsome and mature young man unexpectedly appeared on the horizon and introduced himself as Cezary Kiewra. A few months later, after the preliminary mission of seeking the counsel of the pastor, he asked Łucja for her hand in marriage, and she agreed. God answered her prayer and gave her the husband she desired.

Józef saw the young Kiewra as an answer to his daughter's prayer. He took the whole situation as an unexpected miracle. This event deepened his faith in God and led him to dedicate his whole life to Christ.

His second daughter, Teresa, married Stefan Kuśnierz, who later became the pastor of the church in Lwówek Śląski. Józef's heart was calmed. He became convinced that God was able to take care of even such matters as finding husbands for his daughters.

Social rejection

The most painful thing that Łucja remembered from that period was the rejection that she felt because of her conversion and joining the Pentecostal Church. The society then was not very tolerant toward religious minorities. Members of these minorities were often called "heretic" and their faith, "heretic's faith." Everyone who was not Catholic was treated badly.

Łucja experienced her conversion very deeply. It was such a big blessing for her that she started to tell everyone, in spite of the rejection she experienced. She spoke about Christ, the Gospel, and the Bible. She also gave out Bibles to those who wanted to accept them. Unfortunately, she was often met with negative reactions. People laughed at her, mocked and ridiculed her, and called her, too, a heretic.

When services were held at the Pentecostal Church in Lwówek, no one had enough courage to sit next to the church windows because, at any time, a rock or brick could be thrown from the street and hurt those gathered there. Additionally, people stood outside and loudly shouted and whistled during the services.

This conflict and persecution had a general nature while, to a lesser extent, it moved to personal relations. People teased the Pentecostals' religious diversity but also respected them, seeing that they led a life of righteousness.

The communist authorities in the area also made it difficult though, for a while, they pretended to favor the Pentecostal Church. Reluctantly, the authorities viewed all minority churches as a counterbalance to the Catholic Church, which the Polish communists greatly feared.

From Lubań to Lwówek Śląski by Gryfów Śląski is about 19 miles
Before the marriage with Łucja, Cezary covered this route every Sunday on the bike

The wedding of Cezary and Łucja, 1959

From the left, Olga with little Łucja and sister in Zdolbuniv, 1938

Olga's funeral, Lipsk, June 1945

Łucja's baptism, baptized by Bishop Józef Czerski, Wrocław, 1955

Teresa's baptism, baptized by Walenty Dawidów, Lwówek Śląski, 1956

Andrew Mytych

First from the left, Pastor Eugeniusz Hrycyna, church in Lwówek Śląski, 1958

**Józef Ciechanowski (first from the left)
and friends from work**

Józef Ciechanowski's baptism, Płóczka River, 1958

Józef Ciechanowski's baptism, 1958

(Sitting) Emmie and Józef, (standing) Łucja, Cezary, and Teresa, 1959

Andrew Mytych

5

Tailor, preacher, smuggler

Life and ministry in communist Poland

Ministry for God

After finding believers and joining the church in Lwówek Śląski, Cezary very quickly and with dedication became involved in ministry. He often sang in Russian the Christian songs he had learned in the East, taught the Word of God, and diligently served God and the believers. People really liked him because he was a wise man who was experienced in life. Many, both believers as well as those outside the church fellowship, enjoyed listening to him.

In 1959, the pastor, Eugeniusz Hrycyna ("eh-oo-GEHN-yoosh hrih-TSIH-nah") resigned from pastoring the church. The continual commuting from Legnica had become very burdensome. In anguish, he one day said to the congregation, "I see now that my mission among you has reached the end. God has given you a mature brother in Christ, Cezary Kiewra. He will take care of you. I can peacefully leave my ministry in this church because I know that the mission of the church will be continued."

Cezary decided to develop his life in two areas: in the ministry as well as professionally. On the one hand, he devoted himself to preaching; on the other hand, to tailoring. On December 6, 1959, he was elected as a member of the Council of Elders, and Stefan Kuśnierz, his brother-in-law, became pastor of the church.

In light of the law at that time, the church was treated by the communistic government as an "association" and, therefore, subject to various regulations. The highest authority was the general meeting of members. It was this assembly, and not the leaders, who had the decisive voice through usually secret, democratic voting. The decisions were verified annually because the voice of the people of the church was dominating. Very often, the most active at such meetings were people who, on a daily basis, were not very noticeable. Sometimes their behavior was "inspired" by the authorities. Every official letter had to be signed by the pastor (called "the church superior" at that time), the church's secretary, as well as a member of the Church Council. If it concerned finances, the signature of the treasurer (who was also a member of the Church Council) was additionally required. Officially, Cezary became secretary and Stefan, the church superior.

Life in Lwówek Śląski

After marrying Łucja, Cezary and she moved in with her father into a 3-room apartment. Cezary and Łucja occupied one room, the second belonged to his father-in-law, and the third was used by Teresa with her husband Stefan. After a year, Teresa and Stefan moved to live with his parents.

In January 1960, Łucja gave birth to a daughter, Irena ("ih-REH-na"). In December 1961, Marek ("MAH-rek") came into the world.

In his father-in-law's apartment, Cezary adapted a room in the attic for a tailor's workshop, and he set up the sewing machine brought with him those years before when in Wikszniany. His work day usually started at 5 or 6 o'clock in the morning and ended somewhere between 6 and 9 o'clock at night. He worked hard in this small workshop in the attic until his retirement.

Also in 1962, he completed a 400-hour preparation course for the tailor apprentice and master examinations. At the end of the year, he passed the master's examination in Wrocław for men's tailoring: custom, civil, and uniforms. With pride, he had finally become a certified tailor!

This certification was the next step and one of the most important events in his career as a tailor. Having begun his career in this laborious, but creative profession as a teenager in 1948 while living in the village of Wikszniany, he eventually worked as an apprentice for a master tailor after his post-war relocation to Lubań. However, in Lwówek Śląski, Cezary started a completely new phase in his career. He had his own workshop and, as a craftsman, belonged to the Guild of Tailors.

Slowly, systematically, and because of quality work and reliability, he obtained customers. In the beginning, he lowered his price for services. Although he maintained his official rates in the Chamber of Crafts where his business was registered, he sewed for lesser rates. He did not hesitate to take alterations and, in contrast to certain tailors working in the area, he was honest—he never stole materials that were entrusted to him by his clients!

For example, when he received an order to make a coat for a client, he either returned the leftover material or made an additional piece of clothing. Other tailors did not return the remaining fabric. The delighted women who brought things for sewing eagerly asked him, "How do you do, it Mr. Kiewra? I ordered a coat, and you also have sewn for me a skirt, vest, and hat! That other tailor took the same amount of fabric as you, but *they* didn't give anything back!"

People liked his integrity and his respectful attitude toward customers. He never advertised. He had no need to. Friends and relatives enthusiastically recommended his business to others because he was a skilled, diligent, and honest professional.

Customers came from all over to order suits and dresses. They even came from as far away as Wrocław to have a coat or uniform made. Throughout all the years of his work as a tailor, he never had any complaints or grievances!

A man of principles

From the time of his new birth in the Siberian labor camp, Cezary was a man steadfast and faithful to his principles and values. He was a man of integrity who never compromised, the basis of his conduct being honesty and respect for others. Aside from that, he kept himself very busy. He believed that a man should work to support his family in order to ensure them a quality life.

Fidelity to his wife was an *absolute* principle not subject to any discussion. He was never unfaithful to Łucja. He loved her very much and had a strong sense of loyalty as well as a strong fear of

God. Although opportunities for betrayal were many, "unfaithfulness" was not found in his vocabulary. Women considered Cezary to be a handsome man and, during his work as a tailor, various opportunities availed themselves. A tailor works alone and, as is expected, something needs to be shortened here.... a tuck is needed here.... a side needs to be basted here.... Unintentionally, a part of a woman's body is touched.

One time, their 13-year-old daughter Irena picked up the telephone to secretly eavesdrop on her parents. The Kiewras had two telephones connected to one number on the same line. One phone was in the house, and the second was in Cezary's workshop.

"Hello, Mr. Kiewra here." Irena heard the voice of her confident father in the receiver.

A woman introduced herself and started to speak: "Mr. Kiewra, I'm going to a sanatorium so that I will feel and look better, and it would be great if you would come with me. I will be there by myself, and I would like for you to keep me company. I think you understand what I mean."

Without hesitation, Cezary replied, "No, Ma'am. I will not go with you to the sanatorium. Neither will I meet with you. I am faithful to my wife; I love her and our children. I do not intend to do anything that could harm them. If I am to go anywhere, it will only be with my wife!"

Bible smuggling

In the 1960s and 1970s, Cezary and Łucja often traveled to the East. In Belarus, they visited where Cezary grew up and, in Ukraine, they went to the town where Łucja was born. Cezary also traveled to

Ukraine to see Aurel Serafinczan, his spiritual father from the days of the Gulag. Each time when the Kiewras went on a journey, they took Bibles with them because they were extremely scarce in the Soviet Union. In those times, people entering the soviet republics could take only one copy of the Holy Bible for personal use. Of course, the Kiewras took many more than just the one and successfully managed to smuggle and distribute Bibles over the eastern border.

During his travels, Cezary ministered in illegal services in Pentecostal house churches. In addition to ministry, he didn't waste time, often sewing elegant clothes for the believers for free. His friends on the other side of the eastern border remembered him as a tailor, preacher, and smuggler. When he showed up with that warm smile on his face, he immediately captured the hearts of the people and obtained their favor.

On one of the trips to Belarus in 1973, the Kiewras took their two children, Marek and Irena. Cezary never gave Łucja Bibles to smuggle across the border because when she saw a customs officer, she immediately turned as red as a beet! This usually resulted in her being searched. Cezary knew that children at the border were not subject to border control, so he resolutely girdled them with a belt filled with small Bibles, packed neatly in a row, under their clothes and in the small of their backs. The rest he carried in his own baggage.

During this particular trip, he decided to go to Wikszniany, to his home village. The poverty they saw was overwhelming, especially for Irena and Marek! It appeared that time had stopped and that people had lived for several generations without much change. A muddy road ran through the village, and children ran on it barefooted. One of the barefoot girls was wearing a ragged dress, sewn from material used for making potato sacks. Most families had many children. Women worked hard on the communistic collective farms while men made moonshine in their homes. The concern for life and support of the families rested on the shoulders of the women. It appeared that, in this village, women were created for bearing and rearing children. But their role was not limited to that only because they also had to cook, clean, and make money. Men, however, led a carefree lifestyle. Only a few worked, but certainly almost every one of them drank!

The Kiewras had wanted to visit their family in Wikszniany, but the main purpose of their visit was to share the Good News with the residents. They befriended families. Cezary told those gathered about what God had done in his life and then shared the Word of God with them. He was still known throughout the village, and people were very interested in the history of his life. He also gave to them some of the smuggled Bibles while the other copies he gave to Janinka, who took care of the Christians from Wikszniany. (Cezary had become friends with Janinka after returning from the Siberian labor camp. He had spent many hours with this man in joint prayer.)

The smuggled Bibles were a unique, precious gift. Janinka quietly distributed them among the believers because, unfortunately, many of them did not have a Bible. This Book was a hard-to-get rarity during this time in the Soviet Union.

In addition to sharing the gospel in homes, Cezary also preached sermons. He spoke both to believers as well as to non-believers who secretly came to Janinka to listen to Cezary. While Cezary ministered, Janinka circled around the house, closely observing whether or not someone from the KGB (the feared USSR State Security Committee) was lurking about to spy on them.

The KGB had informers everywhere, and someone very easily could suffer because of their faith in Christ. If someone converted who was an educated person, he usually lost his job and social status. In the documents would be written, *believer.* As a result, no one wanted to hire him for "better" work. Being marked in such a way, employment was only possible on collective farms or as a poorly-paid, low-level worker.

In the Siberian labor camp, Cezary had experienced what it meant to have only one copy of the Bible for every 16 people. Providing Bibles to Belarus and Ukraine was one of the main purposes of Cezary's trips.

Once, when bringing a larger-than-normal amount of Bibles to Ukraine, the Kiewras were caught at the border. In answering the custom officer's questions as to their illegal baggage, Cezary answered, "My wife and I always carry a Bible!"

"Yes, Mr. Kiewra. You may have a Bible, but not several dozen."

The Bibles were confiscated and sent to the Jelenia Góra ("Yeh-LEH-nyah GOOR-ah") Security Service (the Polish secret police during the communistic times). After returning home, Cezary was visited by officers and told to report for questioning to their local headquarters in Jelenia Góra.

They asked him, "What are you doing? How are you doing it? Why are you doing it?" Cezary was not afraid of them and never hid his faith and ministry. Speaking with the secret security agents he said, "My greatest concern is for people to come to faith and receive the Word of God. The Bible is the foundation of faith and without faith, it is impossible to be fully human."

Finally, after several interrogations, he was instructed that what he was doing was wrong and violated the law. They strictly prohibited him from smuggling Bibles to the Soviet Union and left him in peace. Of course, the next time he crossed the eastern border, he took hidden Bibles!

Sometime later, Cezary received from Jelenia Góra the previously-confiscated Bibles. It was not explained to him as to why he received them. Maybe something in the regime changed or they simply cleaned out the warehouse!

The further fate of Aurel

In 1956, after completing a 7-year sentence in the labor camps in Komi ASSR, Aurel Serafinczan returned home to Chernivtsi where he had lived with his parents. Despite warnings from KGB officers, he immediately engaged in church ministry, preaching at illegal home church services and directing the illegal choir.

Music and choir ministry were Aurel's great passions which were instilled in his heart in childhood by his school's music teacher. In addition, his father Mikolaj Serafinczan was an extremely talented man. Before serving his sentence in the labor camp in Irkutsk, he had overseen the development of Christian choirs in Bukovina.

Aurel traveled very often with his choir which performed at illegal church services as well as wedding ceremonies. In connection with this, he brought poverty on himself a number of times.

৯ও৹ ৯ও৹ ৯ও৹ ৯ও৹ ৯ও৹

In Chernivtsi, he was able to get work as a packager in a metal processing factory. In those times, believers who were convicted for being anti-Soviet did not have any chance for better-paid work.

৯ও৹ ৯ও৹ ৯ও৹ ৯ও৹ ৯ও৹

In 1959, he married Minadora, the widow of a Soviet soldier who was killed on the front at the end of World War II. She belonged to the choir where Aurel was the conductor. After getting married, he moved into his wife's home and dedicated the rest of his life to the development of the Pentecostal Church in the Chernivtsi region.

৯ও৹ ৯ও৹ ৯ও৹ ৯ও৹ ৯ও৹

Aurel did not forget about his "sheaves" in the Gulag, about the brothers from Komi ASSR who were part of God's purpose in his life. They regarded him as their spiritual father, and he treated them as his spiritual sons. He regularly corresponded with each of them, and some were guests in his home in Chernivtsi, coming from Belarus and Ukraine. Several times, Cezary Kiewra visited his closest friend and spiritual father.

Aurel also *visited* his spiritual sons. He ministered in churches in Ukraine and Romania, and he also traveled to Poland where, in several cities, he preached the Good News.

❧❧ ❧❧ ❧❧ ❧❧ ❧❧

Daily, Aurel would get up to pray from midnight to three in the morning. But in his old age he thought to himself, "I've grown old. I'm well off in years. I've lost strength. I think that I can stop now getting up at night to pray."

Then, one day brothers from Romania came to a prayer meeting at his house. During prayer, the Holy Spirit spoke through one of them: "You, why have you stopped praying? After all, I hear your prayers!"

The men looked around at each other, not knowing to whom these words were addressed. After a moment of consternation, they continued to pray. When the men finished and prepared to leave, Aurel stopped them. "Brothers, I have something to confess to you," he said. "That word was directed to me. I wanted to stop my nightly prayer because I thought that I am too old for it and now I can relax. I thought that it was time for the young. But now I see that God is waiting for my prayers. He not only hears, but He also answers my prayers. Therefore, I will continue to pray nightly."

❧❧ ❧❧ ❧❧ ❧❧ ❧❧

Aurel Serafinczan died on June 23, 1997, at the age of 75. He was buried in Chernivtsi. He died strong in the faith, having faithfully served God to the end of his life.

And, to the end, he also remembered Cezary Kiewra, his friend and spiritual son.

Cezary and Łucja, Szklarska Poręba

(Sitting from the left) Józef Żuk, in the middle Larysz, on the end, Janika, above him stands Cezary.
In front of the Janika home, 1956, Wikszniany

Cezary Kiewra (second from the left, last row) after a sermon in an illegal church service in the USSR

Aurel (first from the left, kneeling) at an illegal choir practice in the woods, 1967

Хор церкви ХВЄ м. Чернівці, регент
Сарафінчан Аурел

Aurel Serafinczan with his choir in Chernivtsi

Aurel with his wife Minadora

Cezary Kiewra, preacher, in Lwówek Śląski

Cezary, Sunday school teacher, ministering to children;

at the pump organ, Stefan Kuśnierz

Irena and Marek in Lwówek Śląski, 1964

Cezary and Łucja, Marek and Irena, 1965

Andrew Mytych

6

Family

We are only part of a larger whole

Longed-for meeting with father

After many years, Cezary's younger brothers went to England for the long-awaited meeting with their father. One year later, in 1965, Cezary also left for "the Islands." Even in his wildest dreams, Nikodem never thought that it would be 26 years before he would again see his eldest son—and that the reunion would be in Great Britain!

Cezary went to one of the Dutch ports and, from there, sailed to England. Nikodem met him at the port in the southeastern city of Harwich, and they then traveled by train to the large, northeastern city of Bradford.

What a meeting that was! They talked the whole way, unable to get enough of each other. Besides, how is it possible to catch up on 26 years of life? How can you express your happiness about being reunited? How can you express your pain because of the years that were stolen from you?

Cezary spent 3 months in the United Kingdom. During that time, he made a little extra money in his profession. Also, because many people from Poland and Ukraine had immigrated to Bradford after the war, he was able to find some believing Ukrainian immigrants who met in a house church there. Sometimes he would go to services in Leeds, about 13 miles away. Sometimes, he went to Ashton where there was a large Ukrainian church. He quickly became involved in the work of the local Slavic community as a preacher. The local believers liked him so much that they proposed that he move with his family to the United Kingdom and become the pastor of the Slavic church. But he refused because he believed that God had called him to devote himself to ministry in Poland. He knew that Poland was his destiny.

Three months passed very quickly and it was time to part, to return to his wife and children, his small tailoring business, as well as his ministry for God in communist Poland. (Cezary did travel a few more times to the United Kingdom, ministering as a preacher in the local Russian-speaking fellowship.)

Pastoral work in Lubań

In the early 1960s, the church in Lwówek Śląski started a mission post in Lubań, and Jan Lusiński ("YAHN loo-SHEEN-skee") was chosen as its director. In order to support this work, Stefan Kuśnierz, Cezary, and Jan Płachciak ("YAHN PWAH-chyak") rode their bikes from Lwówek to Lubań for the meetings. As a result of their dedicated work, the group of believers in Lubań grew steadily until, finally, it was transformed into a church. However, Jan Lusiński decided to go to another city when things did not work out as time went on. It was then decided that the missionary post in Lubań would be taken over by Cezary, and he would be the pastor of this small church.

Cezary started the hard work of reuniting the people and created a community, its core being made up of believers repatriated from the East. Later, other people converted, joining their brothers and sisters in Christ.

Initially, the believers met in a private home, and then they rented a building from the Evangelical Church. When they were later refused the rented space, one of the Communist parties rented them their hall. The services were very simple, and there were no musical instruments. The faithful sang *a cappella* from the "Pilgrim's Songbook," and then two or three brothers shared the Word of God. Like many pastors in Poland at this time, Cezary had no formal theological preparation. He was, nevertheless, a wise man. He understood how the truth of the Bible could be used in everyday life, which is why a practical dimension could always be perceived in his sermons.

Cezary's ministry was predominantly pastoral. He believed that a pastor is, first and foremost, called to care for the "sheep," the people who follow after the Great Shepherd, Jesus Christ. For this reason, he devoted a lot of time to visiting people in their homes and inviting a few people from the congregation for dinner every Sunday. Another important element of his ministry was prayer. Every day, he shut himself in his tailor's workshop for 2 or 3 hours of peace and concentration in order to read the Bible and seek the face of God. He fasted often because he believed that only through fasting and fervent prayer could a foundation be laid for a good life and ministry, as well as fighting for God's blessing for one's children. He spent *hours* on his knees before God, interceding for the church and his loved ones.

Cezary served as pastor of the Lubań church until he retired in the late 1980s. The role of pastor of the church was then passed to his son-in-law, Karol Staniec ("KAH-rol STAHN-yets").

Nikodem returns to Poland

In 1972, Cezary's 65-year-old father became severely ill. Cezary immediately flew to the United Kingdom to visit him. Two years later, after Nikodem had recovered from an operation, Cezary and Łucja traveled to Bradford and took him back to Poland.

Nikodem had decided to return to his homeland because of sickness and age, but he also had a great longing for Poland and family. Nikodem had many worries and much anguish because of his son Adam, a prodigal who squandered money on alcohol and horse racing. He could not bear to see how his wealth, which he had worked so very hard for, melted away before his eyes. Adam's irresponsible lifestyle shattered their family. Mother often tried to hide it from father and secretly gave him money for his addictions.

During the years spent in emigration, Nikodem had gradually multiplied his wealth. He started in 1945 by running a repair company, specializing in roof and chimney repairs. With time, in addition to managing his company, he decided to buy a few rental homes and rent out apartments. Then he extended his activities. He purchased homes, repaired them, and sold them. Having started "from scratch," he gradually acquired a large fortune which, to his great dismay, was systematically being squandered by his youngest son. What he had accumulated from years of hard work as an émigré would eventually be completely lost.

Nikodem wanted to spend his old age close to Cezary who acted very differently from Adam. Cezary worked a lot, did not drink, and took care of his family. Nikodem and Wiktoria also decided that they wanted to die near their oldest son. So, they bought the unfinished half of a duplex in Lwówek and moved there in 1978, joined by Cezary and his family.

Nikodem was a righteous, honest, and very hard-working man. Men who did not work as much as he thought they should always irritated him. Nearing the end of his life and because of poor health, he complained that he could not work. Sometimes his family caught him shoveling snow from one pile to another. Cezary told him, "Dad, after all, the sun will melt it all! Why are you toiling with this?"

Angrily, Nikodem answered, "You had better go and take care of your own business!" And then he returned to the shoveling. He was a stubborn man. If he decided on something, it was hard to dissuade him from his decision.

At the end of his life, Nikodem was diagnosed with terminal leukemia. Blood transfusions given in Lwówek Śląski's hospital were extending his life to some degree. But one day, in agony, he said to Cezary, "Cezary, my son, I do not want to live. Look at me! See what I look like! I am a living corpse. I don't want any more transfusions. Do not take me for treatments anymore. My time has come. I want to leave!"

When the treatments were discontinued, his state of health deteriorated dramatically from day to day. Cezary, seeing that Nikodem was feeling much worse and being aware that he only had a few hours remaining—at most, a few days—went to his father, sat beside him and said, "Dad, we all have to die and depart from this world. Not all of us, though, are ready to meet our Creator. Would you like for me to pray for you? Do you want to entrust your life to Christ?" Nikodem confirmed by nodding his head. Cezary took him by the hand and led him in a prayer of repentance and thanksgiving. Nikodem closed his eyes, very touched by the prayer of his son, and gave his life to God. A few days later, Wiktoria woke Cezary during the night. "Son, your father has passed away!"

On September 25, 1981, Nikodem died at the age of 77. Wiktoria passed away four years later. They were buried as they had wished, in Lwówek Śląski. *In Poland!*

The tragic fate of Cezary's brothers

Cezary's brothers enjoyed drinking. Such were the times, and a lot of alcohol was drunk then. It became an integral part of life for Poles.

Cezary, as a believer, did not drink or party, thus giving rise to dissatisfaction and taunting from his brothers. They were disappointed in his lifestyle. When talking to him, they said things—but were really unaware of what they were saying.

"Oh, Cezary. You joined your life with those Baptists! You'll die of boredom. Hey, Brother, you need to drink with us! Enjoy the world while you are still young!"

To this Cezary steadfastly answered, "Guys, if you are going to live and drink so stupidly, for certain you will go to the grave faster than I. Because of your foolish lifestyles, you will die before I do!"

They only laughed at him but, undaunted, Cezary constantly repeated, "Brothers, give your lives to God. Repent and start to live properly."

Wiktor died first, in June 1966, at the age of 31. One day during a storm, he was returning home drunk from a family party. While cycling across a bridge, he hit another cyclist, fell off his bike, and hit his head on the curb. As a result of this terrible accident, he suffered traumatic skull and brain injury. He lived less than a week and left three small children, ages 4, 6, and 8.

In 1978, at the age of 45, Janek died of a heart attack. He was a good car mechanic, specializing in auto-body repair. People who asked talented professionals for various favors got them drunk, bringing them alcohol as payment for services. This was one of the reasons why many professionals fell into alcoholism during communist times, and Janek was no exception. He was a drinker. He was often in such a state of drunkenness that, in delirium, he saw horses pulling a carriage on wires. His life revolved around the bottles. He even slept with them. Shortly before his death, he stopped drinking because he started to feel very bad. Sadly, they didn't take him to a hospital in time.

In 1999, Adam died of larynx cancer at the age of 61 in Bradford, England. In the beginning of his time in Great Britain, he worked with his father. Then he became independent and ran his own company, doing work that he learned from his dad. Everything would have worked out fine if he hadn't been drinking daily. This habit, along with an addiction to gambling on horse races, led to ultimate tragedy. At the end of his life, he was tormented with the addictions and deep loneliness. His final years were spent in extreme poverty, and his last apartment resembled a dark burrow. A single light bulb hung from the ceiling, and an old quilt lay across the bed on which were no linens.

It turned out that Cezary, although the eldest, survived them all.

Golden Anniversary

Cezary and Łucja have lived together as a couple for more than 50 years, always a testimony to family and friends of a good, happy marriage. They have been an example and proof that one can live a normal, fulfilled life in accordance with biblical values and dedication to God.

In September 2009, they marked their Golden Anniversary. Cezary and Łucja, together with four generations of Kiewras and friends, celebrated and thanked God for half a century of His blessings and abundance. God gave Cezary the possibility to enjoy a long life. He has seen his children, grandchildren, and great-grandchildren. His son Marek walks in his father's footsteps and preaches the Good News. He completed his theological studies in Warsaw, planted a church in a city near Lwówek, and became its pastor. Cezary stressed that Marek had reached a place in the ministry where he, during his times of pastoring, never even *thought* possible.

Bradford, Great Britain; standing from the left, Cezary, Adam's wife, Adam; Sitting, Wiktoria with grandson Mirosław (Adam's son) and Nikodem

Cezary Kiewra, pastor of the church in Lubań,
March 17, 1969

Ordination of Cezary Kiewra as presbyter;
At the pulpit, presbyter Teodor Maksymowicz

Cezary (kneeling) ordained as presbyter by presbyter Sergiusz Waszkiewicz, assisted by presbyters Teodor Maksymowicz and Aleksander Mankowski, Lwówek Śląski, 1973

Andrew Mytych

Family gathering, Bradford, Great Britain, 1964;from the left, Wiktor (2 years before he died), Janek, and Adam

Golden anniversary of Cezary and Łucja, 2009

**Family celebrating the golden anniversary
of Cezary and Łucja, 2009**

7

In his father's footsteps

In his early childhood and youth, Marek Kiewra, the only son of Cezary and Łucja, did not measure up to the expectations of others. He lacked confidence and was very shy. He was often distracted and unable to focus his attention on anything for very long. He was also light-hearted.

Some shook their heads in disbelief, wondering how it was possible that *"the apple fell so far from the tree"*! Why was he not like his father? People found it difficult to believe that he could ever walk in his father's footsteps and do something worthwhile in life. His father, however, was not discouraged by what he saw or by what people said. He knew that God, Whom he faithfully served, could do anything and that He had the power to straighten the winding roads of his son. In his youth, Cezary himself was far from the ideal, so he did not worry too much about Marek's antics. He trusted him and believed that he would prosper in life and grow up to be a good man. He also expected that his son would experience God's extraordinary blessing. Therefore, almost daily, he knelt before God and prayed for his son, convinced that everything would work out well.

Even in his childhood, Marek had a strong inner conviction that God was calling him to the ministry. During a conversation with his grandmother Emmie, he first became aware of his calling. One day she unexpectedly asked, "My Dear, who would you like to be? What would you like to do in life when you grow up?"

"I would like to serve God," he said without a moment's thought, surprised at his own words.

"Marek, that is the best choice!" replied his grandmother with a radiant face.

This inner conviction about his calling did not leave him. A few years later, when in high school, he wondered about which university he should go to upon graduation, what direction he should take. Again this thought was dominating: He felt that he should apply to a theology school in Warsaw to begin preparations for the ministry. It was a turning point in his life.

Five years of studies at the Christian Theological Academy deepened his passion for the Word of God and his interest in ministry. One day, while praying with other students and then talking about what each would like to do in the future, he said, "I would like to plant a church in a small Polish town, starting from scratch. I think that God is calling me to pioneering missionary work." It became the subject of his thoughts and prayer requests.

While in Warsaw, there developed the desire to go somewhere to get *practical* experience in order to learn something more than what he had obtained in his home church in Lwówek Śląski. Although he had received solid theological and theoretical preparation from the Warsaw university, he also wanted see how others built churches and proclaimed the Word of God. He learned English with the conviction that he should become fluent for it would be necessary to fulfill his calling.

When he was in the third or fourth year of his studies, some students from *Christ for the Nations* Bible school in Dallas, Texas, came to his university in Warsaw and brought Polish Bibles. He was their guide. He found out that the school had interesting classes on practical ministry, and going there would also provide an excellent opportunity for mastering his English. In addition, it had a scholarship program that allowed persons from communist and developing countries to study for almost free. He submitted an application to the school and was granted admission.

He studied in Dallas from 1987 to 1988. It was an exceptional year in his life. He had the opportunity to practice ministry and to improve his English. It also significantly expanded his horizons. He fell in love with the United States. But, he knew that his *calling* was to Poland. He nurtured in his heart that desire to plant a church in a small, almost rural town where there was still no evangelical church.

Moreover, calling him back to the country was his longing for Wanda ("VAHN-da") with her big blue eyes. She was the love of his life! And she was waiting for him in his hometown. It turned out that he was the first student from Poland at *Christ for the Nations* who, after graduation, did not stay in the U.S. but returned to his country to serve God.

❦ ❦ ❦ ❦ ❦

He had met Wanda before departing for his studies in Warsaw. He liked very much this assertive and resolute girl, and they started dating before he left for the United States. The separation was a difficult test that deepened their feelings. They wrote to each other and sometimes also called.

After returning from the United States, he asked for her hand in marriage on June 6, 1988. Since she was 24 years old at the time, he handed her a bouquet of 24 tea roses! In October of the same year, they took their vows. Later, they became the parents of two sons, Paul and Peter.

Wanda has significantly contributed to Marek's success in life. He quickly avows that he would not be who he is if it were not for his wife. This was noticed very early on by Michał Hydzik ("MEE-khow HIH-jik"), the Bishop of the Pentecostal Church at the time. During Marek's ordination, he solemnly said, "You are who are you because of your wife's contribution."

Wanda supported Marek in the pastoral ministry and gave him a lot of "space," not making excuses because of the many, and sometimes too long, foreign trips. Over time, she became more involved in ministering to women. This resulted in her eventually becoming director of the Polish branch of the international women's ministry, *Aglow,* in 2009. This is an association that encourages ordinary women, regardless of denomination, skin color, or origin to carry the message of God's love to all the places where it has not yet reached.

❧❧ ❧❧ ❧❧ ❧❧ ❧❧

Before leaving in 1987 for study in the United States, Marek was already involved in the preaching ministry in the church in Lwówek Śląski and surrounding towns. One of the towns was Gryfów Śląski ("GRIH-foof SHLOHN-skee"), located 11 miles from Lwówek. There was a house group there that, during his studies in the U.S., was led by several brothers from the Lwówek church. Wanda, who later became his wife, also went here.

After returning from the States, Marek helped Stefan Kuśnierz (who was still pastoring the church in Lwówek), and he traveled to Lubań and Zgorzelec, as well. He was also involved in organizing many evangelistic events in nearby towns. Finally, he was prepared and ready to lead the church in Gryfów Śląski. He and Wanda met regularly to pray with a few Christians. They prayed persistently and systematically. The women kept a prayer log and prayed for the salvation of specific people, for revival in the town, and the creation of a strong church.

In the beginning of the church, 11 women converted. Marek couldn't accept such a reality. Therefore, he often prayed to God, *"Lord God, I am only to be blessed among women? I need men! I need young people! I need children! I would like to care for a church that has all the generations! Hear my request and increase this church!"*

The prayer was combined with numerous evangelistic activities. The planting of the church also coincided with the fall of communism in Poland, and Poles were extremely receptive and open to new trends, concepts, philosophies, and religions. Mass evangelism attracted crowds. So, he invited many different mission groups, music bands, and evangelists and showed Christian films.

The Gospel was preached in the main square, in the city center, at the cultural center, in the cinema, in bars, on the streets, in private homes, and even in the schools. Soon people began to convert, and the core of the church was established.

Twice a week, he conducted house groups and also rented the Senior Club where he conducted the first service. In 1990, he leased a furniture warehouse in a building that had been a German winery. The church adapted the hall for religious purposes. By the grace of God and the favor of the people, he began to buy sections of the building until the *entire* building became the property of the church. He and the church members made the necessary renovations to meet the needs of the developing fellowship.

Although many new people came to the church meetings, it was difficult in the beginning to "start" the church. This was because there were no mature Christians and, in particular, no mature leaders who could carry part of the leadership burden as well as be a part of the church formation process. For years he prayed for leaders and a leadership team, and God gradually began sending him workers.

Kenneth Hevreyen, a missionary from Australia, helped him for a year. Kenneth came to Poland with a bus equipped for the needs of evangelism. (His story is described in the book, *Living Stones*.) Thanks to his ministry, many people in Gryfów Śląski experienced a meeting with God.

Throughout this entire time, Marek prayed to discover the direction that his work should take in Gryfów Śląski. He kept feeling that he was missing something important, but he didn't know what it was. One morning, God unexpectedly spoke to him. After finishing morning intercessory prayer with a group of believers, he drove around the square several times, asking God for the salvation of people, revival in the area, and the creation of a strong church in this small, provincial Polish town. (He had regularly driven down the streets and prayed, looking at houses and pedestrians. Daily he saw people who, from early morning, were already completely intoxicated.)

This particular day, the sight of these people on the gray sidewalks of Gryfów completely broke his heart. Deeply moved by the pathetic state of these addicted people and their families, he began to cry out to God: "Oh, Lord God, touch these people! Perform a miracle! Change their lives!"

Then he heard a voice: "YOU do it!"

Immediately, he stopped the car, went to the sidewalk, and began to talk with a drunken man. This was the unexpected beginning of the New Hope ministry through which God later touched many addicts and their families. That day he understood that he should reach out to these people. Initially, he had no idea about how to do it. He had no training in this area. But, although he did not know *what* to do, he understood that, most likely, the key to success for a breakthrough and the church's eventual success was dealing with the main problem of the town's residents whom he decided to serve.

Soon afterwards, Andrzej Kurzawsk ("AHND-zhay KOO-zhafsk") showed up at the Gryfów church. God had delivered him from alcoholism and given him a strong love for people enslaved to addiction. Andrzej became the leader of New Hope. Shortly afterwards, his assistance (together with other leaders whom God added to the church) helped the church develop, and the Good News reached many of the lost, including those living on the margins of life. Today, Gryfów Śląski's church members are people who were alcoholics, drug addicts, homeless, criminals, and mafia thugs. God gave them grace. He stretched out His hands and freed them.

For the 9 years following Bible school in the United States, Marek was focused mainly on the development of the local church in Gryfów. During this time, he did little travel, devoting himself to pastoral work, organizing evangelistic events, and providing charitable aid. Marek also arranged the transport of used clothing and hospital equipment from abroad. He did not expect that the Lord would also call him to preach the Word of God in other countries.

Looking back to Marek's early years, it was rather difficult to consider the first sermon he ever preached as an example of great oratory. When Marek was 16 years old, Pastor Kuśnierz said to him, "Today you will preach a sermon at the evening service."

"Okay," he answered uncertainly.

The rest of the day he sat nervously at home, his mind a complete blank. In his thoughts was only one paralyzing question:

"What am I to say today? What am I to say today?" Panic was growing in his heart!

Finally, his mother came to his aid. "Son, read chapter 14 of the Gospel of John," she said with a smile.

"All right, Mom, I'll do it," he said with a little less uneasiness.

That evening, he stood in the church pulpit, opened the Bible, and said solemnly, "My Path to the Father." Then, following his mother's advice, he read the afore-mentioned fragment of the gospel.

When he finished reading, people looked at him curiously, expecting his continuation. But he only added, "And so we should all do the same. Amen!" With that, he left the pulpit and sat in the pew. That was probably the most succinct sermon in the history of that church!

Many years have passed since then. He has preached thousands of sermons. In 1997, 9 years after graduating from *Christ for the Nations*, Marek returned for the first time to the United States to preach the Word of God. From that moment on, he has preached the Word in that country at least once a year. He also has ministered in many European countries and gone to Canada, Brazil, and even Mali. He ministers at various conferences and conventions, in churches, and at meetings for men and businessmen. He likes to speak on missions, being convinced that everyone has something to contribute to this important ministry.

Over time, a strong vision was born in his heart to build a Christian leisure and training center that churches, pastors, and spiritual leaders from Poland and neighboring countries could use. He carried this vision for many years, dreaming of a place where Christians could experience meetings with God and spiritual renewal, as well as draw inspiration for their continual way of life with Christ.

He didn't know, however, what such a center could look like, where it should be created, or how it should operate. He only knew one thing—he very much wanted to create a place that would have a high standard in all respects and would impact the lives of thousands of people. Year by year his dream became increasingly more real.

A breakthrough came in 2002 when he participated in a meeting of leaders and businessmen at the training center of the Haggai Institute in Hawaii. He saw the comfort of the Center and also noted the high quality of training. This was precisely the type of training center that he wanted to create in Poland, designed for Christians from Central and Eastern Europe. He understood that the region in which God had called him to ministry needed a good Christian center. And, with God's help, he could manage such a task.

Considering all that he had learned in America, he thought to himself, "Why do we Polish pastors and leaders hold our training and conferences in poor conditions? We sleep in 6-person rooms on mattresses or beds which should have been thrown away a long time ago! Why do we return home after a conference more tired than when we left? After all, we Poles need quality, too. We need to begin to do things with much greater class!"

Thanks to his ties with different people and an unexpected series of events, he purchased some beautiful property a few miles from Gryfów Śląski, in a small, quiet village called Karłowice (kar-woh-VEETS-eh"). In 2006, he opened a modern Christian leisure and training center which he called "The Green Pastures."

Today, the center has a life of its own. Christians from Poland, Germany, the Netherlands, Czech Republic, Belarus, the United States, and many other countries come to stay here. People come for training, conferences, conventions, vacations, and retreats. It is a place where Christians have the opportunity to relax, listen to inspiring teaching, meet interesting people, get closer to God, renew their strength, and think about their life. Some even come to this place to write a book! And, aside from all this, the center is used as a base for mission groups that come to Poland.

But, the history of the Center is material for a completely different book which, one day, may be written and, no doubt, *should* be written.

Marek Kiewra in Dallas, Texas, 1988

Marek and Wanda Kiewra

"The Green Pastures" Center in Karłowice

http://zielonaniwa.com/en/green-pastures/

Epilogue

My father

I am very happy that a book has been published about my father, Cezary Kiewra, and his friends. I think that in this way, the fascinating story of God's work in the lives of ordinary people was preserved from being forgotten.

This book is an interesting testimony of those times, presented to readers through the prism of ordinary people's lives. As far as I know, there is a large gap in literature about the life and ministry of Pentecostals in the first half of communist times in Poland. Thanks to this book, the younger generation can become familiar with the harsh reality of this period of history and also learn what it means to dedicate one's life to Christ and serve Him, remaining faithful to Him even in difficult circumstances. The people in this book (and untold others) understood what it means to "count the cost" of following Jesus Christ. At the same time, the older generation will be able to recall their own memorable experiences from that period. And, for the readers who only briefly met my father at some point or have personally known him over the years, this book will have special meaning.

My father's history was dramatic, like most Poles from his generation. As a small boy, he was separated from his father with whom he was very emotionally connected. Then, when he was 19 years old, he was sentenced to 25 years of slave labor for helping the Home Army and then sent to labor camps in Siberia. There, in the raw realities of Stalinist times, he met Christ. This meeting radically changed him! He surrendered to God and, against the difficult circumstances of life, he devoted himself to ministry.

The heroes of faith are described in the Bible letter named "Hebrews." Today, when I reflect on this text, my heroes are not only Abraham, Moses, and the others listed there, but also my father and many people from his generation. Neither Cezary nor Aurel were pastors of large churches during their lives. They did not start large, international parachurch organizations. They did not leave behind huge assets. But I see them as heroes because they trusted God and stood for Him in ruthless, Stalinist times. They decided to serve Him regardless of the price that would need to be paid, and they finished their lives strong in the faith. They valued the ministry that God entrusted to them and faithfully served the best they knew how. For me, they are a model of faith, service, and abiding in God, both in good times and bad. They were our fathers, and we can continue the work of God, building greater things than they did on the foundations that they laid in tears.

The beauty of this book is that it tells a story that does not die with its main heroes. They were part of a larger whole, a part of God's bigger plan that extends from generation to generation. I also ponder this myself and encourage readers to think about the legacy.

After all, this story about my father is really about *passing the Gospel, the Faith, from generation to generation.*

I also believe that this book will inspire many who are either looking for God or who are already following Him. The stories described are rooted in harsh, communist realities, but certain truths and ramifications presented in it are universal and timeless. Here is the message that God, who is presented in the pages of the Bible, is the real and true God who both "finds" a person and allows Himself to be found. Our family knows Him as the One who turns everything around for the good, although the beginnings may sometimes be difficult and incomprehensible. He abundantly blesses those who love Him, from generation to generation.

When I became acquainted with the book during its formation, I asked myself a question: How do I remember my dad from those years? The answer was simple: the same as believers from the East used to call him—*tailor, preacher,* and *smuggler.* Tailoring was the love of his life. He was an honest and skilled craftsman. But far more important was his passion for ministry. Under the communist political realities of that time, pastors had to have secular occupations. They could not devote themselves to only pastoral work. While working as a tailor, my dad dedicated his life to pastoral care and preaching. He also found ways to smuggle Bibles into the Soviet Union, *always* showing great respect and love for the *Holy Bible.*

My dad had a major impact on my life. His example inspired me to follow God, and he imparted his devotion to pastoring and preaching. He was a model of patience and sacrifice, faithfully serving God, his family, and church.

He only finished seventh grade of primary school, which was the case for many from his generation. But he was a wise man, experienced in life. As our father, he gave advice to my sister and me. We did not always listen to him. Now I know that if we had been more receptive to what he said, our adult life certainly would have been better.

I also remember him as a man of prayer. My father had a tailoring shop in the tenement building where we lived. When I was a small boy, I would frequently run there. But during the day, there were moments when the workshop door was locked. I didn't know why, and I was always very curious about it.

One day, by accident, the mystery was solved because my father had forgotten to lock the door. As usual, I burst into the workshop; but this time, I saw my dad on his knees. In prayer, he was pouring out his heart and tears to God. His tailor's workshop was also his prayer closet!

I asked, "Dad, what are you doing on your knees?"

"Son," he said, "every day I lock myself in the workshop and for 2 hours I pray to God for myself and for our entire family. I'm praying for you!"

This had an amazing impact on me. The image of my father kneeling daily before God became an inspiring model. And I am convinced that his prayers have had a lasting, positive impact on my life. I believe that I enjoy such great blessings and God's favor in every area today because of who my dad was and what he fought for in his prayer closet.

It is a powerful testimony of what a man of God can do by persevering in his prayer closet!

In my childhood, we always finished the day in a specific way. The entire 3-generation family gathered together in the dining room of the large apartment in which we lived, an apartment that was in an old, formerly German tenement building. My sister sat at the piano and played a song from the "Pilgrim's Songbook." We all sang. My father would then stand, read from the Scriptures, and then we prayed, showing God our gratitude. Every evening we thanked God for what He had done in our lives, as well as for that day. It was something amazing! At the time, I did not understand the importance of those evenings spent with my family in fellowship with God. I was not yet born again. But when I gave my life to God, those evenings took on a special significance. Now I understand how important it is to spend time with God as a family. I am convinced that it is important to start and finish each day in fellowship with Him.

There were other things that, as a child, I did not understand. I did not understand many things about my father's behavior, and some of them seemed completely senseless. For example, when returning from church service on Sundays, dad would invite to our home people who were elderly, single, or walking with crutches, and we ate lunch together with them. I was not happy about it. I remember how often I unhappily wondered, "What is he doing? Why is he doing this? After all, this is completely without any sense. Don't we deserve some free family time?" But now when I look back on those Sundays—my being a man in the prime of life, having also dedicated my life to serving God and people—I admire my parents' dedication. Now I understand that my dad, who is the focus of this story, was led by his sympathy and love for people. He loved to share his time with others and serve them, especially those who were elderly, alone, and somehow wronged by life.

I remember also that when I left for my theological studies in Warsaw, my dad said to me, "I will work more to help you finance your education. I would like very much for you to graduate from the academy as an educated man prepared to serve God."

He finished only seven grades of primary school, and the war and postwar turmoil took away his youth. He knew, though, that education was very important and wanted me to go farther in life and ministry than he did. Just as he promised, he helped provide for my education so that I could serve God as a theologically-educated pastor.

I have been blessed by God to have a good father. He has been an example and inspiration. He cared for me and helped me. I wouldn't be the man I am today if it were not for him. His example is one of the reasons for my choosing *this* path of life and not another. Today, I want to carry the torch that was passed to me—to share God's light with as many people as possible—and to pass on the baton to as many as who will receive it as I run this marathon called the Christian life.

Of course, we can't forget to mention Aurel Serafinczan, the spiritual father of my dad and many other leaders in the Pentecostal movement during communism. In contemporary terminology, we would call him a *mentor*. After returning home from the labor camps, he invited his disciples to his home in Chernivtsi in Bukovina, or he traveled to the countries and republics where *they* lived and served.

I was a small boy when I met him for the first time in Belarus during a visit in which my father was smuggling Bibles to the Soviet Union. Then, later, he came to our home. I was curious about this man because my dad talked about him a lot. My dad reiterated that because of Aurel, his own life was what it was. He eagerly added that if it were not for Aurel, for certain he would not have known Christ as his Lord and Savior. He continued that he also would not have met my mother Łucja, his *Rebecca*. He would not have become a pastor or started a church in Lubań. It's astonishing how much influence some people have on our lives and how significant the consequences are!

Aurel Serafinczan made a strong impression on me. He was a modest man, leading an almost ascetic life. Regardless of where he was, from midnight to three in the morning he prayed, treating prayer as an integral part of his calling. Every time he prayed in a setting where I could hear him, it made a huge impression on me.

When I planted the church in Gryfów Śląski, Aurel came and shared the Word of God. He preached firmly, but with humility. He was a very anointed prophet. I wonder now how he felt when God allowed him, in his old age, to preach in a church founded by the son of his disciple! How satisfying it must be to see the fruit of your work in subsequent generations!

Today, when I reflect on all of this, I can see clearly that, through *one* man and his obedience, the lives of many people— maybe even thousands of people—have been transformed. When God told him in the late 1940s to be prepared for prison and, later, to start an underground church in the labor camps, he could have rebelled. He could have refused God, but he did not resist and did not run away. He didn't make any excuses to God. He calmly surrendered to the leading of the Holy Spirit. By God's grace, he founded an underground church in the labor camp in the far North and, with difficulty, won 15 people for Christ. Then, risking his life, he conducted illegal meetings with them, raising them as disciples of Christ. There he also led my father, Cezary Kiewra, to God and trained him to be a radical Christian. When my dad, repatriated from the East, came to the Recovered Territories in western Poland in the late 1950s, he became involved in the ministry of the church in Lwówek Śląski. Later, he founded the church in Lubań. My father made a big impact on my life and on the lives of many others.

Because of Aurel's obedience all those years ago, today we see the fruit of what God started in the 1940s and 1950s. The legacy that Aurel passed to his disciples continues to be passed along even further. It is alive, and God still is multiplying the fruits of the faithfulness of these men of God.

When I share the Word of God in my country and abroad, I often repeat my conviction:

"Today I stand before you and preach the Word of God because of the obedience of one person. If it were not for this man, Aurel Serafinczan, and his obedience to God, I probably would not be here

now. But because of his obedience and faithfulness, I can today travel to many countries, preach the Word of God, and see the great things that God is doing!"

I am eternally grateful to God and also to the spiritual fathers who walked before me, who sometimes paid an unimaginable price so that I and others can have true life in Jesus Christ.

45373201R00090

Made in the USA
Charleston, SC
21 August 2015